Unlocking the Secrets of
SACRED GEOMETRY

Part I: Foundations of the Divine Pattern

Introduction: Seeing the World Through Sacred Geometry

"Mathematics is the language with which God has written the universe."
— **Galileo Galilei**

We live in a world shaped not only by matter, but by **pattern**—a hidden web of relationships, proportions, and symmetries that bind the seen and unseen together. From the spiral of a seashell to the orbit of planets, from ancient temples to blooming flowers, a universal language speaks through form. This language is **sacred geometry**.

But sacred geometry is not just about shapes and numbers—it's about a way of **seeing**. It's a lens through which we glimpse the intelligence behind creation. When we learn to recognize this pattern, we begin to shift how we perceive the world: not as chaos, but as a meaningful and interconnected whole.

What Is Sacred Geometry, Really?

At its core, sacred geometry is the study of shapes, patterns, and proportions that hold symbolic and energetic significance. It's the bridge between **science and spirit**, **math and mysticism**. The term "sacred" is used not to imply religious dogma, but to point to something **universal**, **archetypal**, and often mysterious—patterns that appear consistently in nature, art, architecture, and spiritual traditions across time and culture.

The spiral of a galaxy mirrors the spiral of a pinecone. The proportions of the Great Pyramid echo the golden ratio found in leaves, seashells, and even your DNA. These are not coincidences. They are part of a deeper order.

A Language Older Than Words

Long before written language, human beings told stories through symbols and geometry. Ancient temples, megaliths, and sacred art carry geometric patterns that reflect cosmological truths. From the **mandalas** of the East to the **kabbalistic Tree of Life**, sacred geometry offered a way to encode wisdom—mathematically precise and spiritually profound.

For the ancients, geometry wasn't merely an academic study—it was a **path to enlightenment**. To draw a circle or trace a pentagram was to participate in the act of creation itself.

Modern Eyes, Ancient Wisdom

Today, science confirms what mystics and builders of sacred sites intuited thousands of years ago: the universe is mathematical. Fractals, golden spirals, waveforms, and vibrational patterns shape the very fabric of existence. With this realization, sacred geometry is being reawakened—not just as ancient knowledge, but as a **living philosophy** for a more harmonious way of being.

To study sacred geometry now is not about nostalgia for the past; it is an invitation to reconnect with our own **inner design**, and the design of the cosmos.

Chapter 2: What Is Sacred Geometry?

"Geometry will draw the soul toward truth and create the spirit of philosophy."
— **Plato**

Sacred geometry is the study of the **fundamental patterns, proportions,** and **shapes** that structure all matter and life in the universe. It is called "sacred" not because the shapes themselves are religious, but because they reflect **universal laws** and **divine intelligence**—the invisible scaffolding upon which reality is built.

To understand sacred geometry is to begin seeing **form as meaning, structure as spirit**, and **pattern as presence**. Whether in the arrangement of petals on a flower, the spiral of a galaxy, or the design of ancient temples, sacred geometry reveals a **deep coherence** connecting the microcosm and macrocosm.

Geometry vs. Sacred Geometry

Traditional geometry is the mathematical study of shapes, sizes, and the properties of space. It's concerned with precision, equations, and logical relationships. Sacred geometry, on the other hand, expands that understanding to include **symbolic, energetic, and philosophical dimensions**. It asks:

- Why do these patterns show up so consistently in nature?
- What do these shapes **mean**?
- How do they reflect the **structure of consciousness, creation**, or **the divine**?

Sacred geometry is **multi-dimensional**. It is at once scientific and spiritual, logical and intuitive, visual and energetic. It speaks to both the **left brain** and the **right brain**, inviting a holistic way of understanding reality.

The Core Idea: Order in Creation

The essence of sacred geometry lies in the idea that **everything in the universe is part of a grand, harmonious design**. This design expresses itself through specific geometric principles and ratios that repeat across scale and form.

Some of these include:

- **The Circle** – unity, infinity, wholeness
- **The Triangle** – balance, trinity, stability
- **The Square** – matter, structure, grounding
- **The Golden Ratio (Φ)** – the proportion of beauty and growth
- **The Fibonacci Sequence** – the pattern of natural expansion
- **Fractals** – self-similar repetition at different scales
- **The Platonic Solids** – elemental forms that underlie all matter

Each of these elements isn't just a shape; it is an **archetype**, a **symbol**, and in many traditions, a **portal to higher understanding**.

A Universal Language Across Time and Culture

What makes sacred geometry so compelling is that it is **cross-cultural and timeless**. Across continents and millennia, civilizations have turned to geometry to symbolize the divine and structure sacred space.

Examples include:

- **The pyramids of Egypt**, built with proportions reflecting golden ratios
- **The Hindu mandalas** and **Buddhist yantras**, using concentric geometry for meditation
- **Gothic cathedrals** in Europe, designed with geometric harmony to uplift the soul
- **Islamic art**, which uses complex geometric patterns to reflect the infinite nature of God
- **Native American medicine wheels**, based on radial symmetry and circular form

Without sharing language or religion, these cultures tapped into **universal truths** expressed through geometry. It suggests that these patterns are not inventions, but **discoveries**—revealed through direct experience of the cosmos.

Geometry in Nature

Sacred geometry isn't confined to human-made structures—it's everywhere in nature:

- **Honeycombs** form hexagonal cells, maximizing efficiency
- **Sunflowers** and **pinecones** grow according to the **Fibonacci sequence**
- **Nautilus shells** and **galaxies** spiral in logarithmic proportions
- **Snowflakes** form radial, symmetrical six-pointed shapes

- **Spiderwebs, waves, tree branches,** and **lightning bolts** all follow fractal patterns

These aren't just aesthetic. They reflect the **efficiency and intelligence of natural design.** Nature follows geometry because it is the most elegant and effective way to grow, distribute energy, and organize form.

More Than Visual – A Vibrational Reality

At its deepest level, sacred geometry is **vibrational.** Every shape has a frequency. Every proportion affects how energy flows. This is why sacred geometry is used in **sound healing, architecture, energy medicine,** and even **quantum physics.**

- The **circle** is the shape of waves and vibrations.
- **Mantras and chants** are geometric in resonance.
- **Cymatics** (the study of sound patterns in matter) shows how vibrations form sacred patterns in sand, water, and other materials.

This suggests that the universe is not only built on **form,** but that **form is a result of vibration**—that the geometry we see is the frozen echo of deeper, unseen forces.

Why It's Sacred

So what makes geometry **sacred**?

It's not the shape itself. It's what the shape **reveals**—about nature, about consciousness, about the infinite intelligence that weaves all things together. Sacred geometry invites us into a space of awe, contemplation, and alignment with something greater than ourselves.

It becomes sacred when we:

- Recognize the **divine intelligence** behind creation
- Feel a **deep harmony** between self and cosmos
- Use these patterns as tools for **healing, transformation,** or **spiritual insight**

- Align our thoughts, homes, bodies, and practices with these universal structures

Sacred geometry is the **architecture of the universe**—a language that communicates through pattern, proportion, and harmony. It is an ancient science, a spiritual practice, a tool for awakening, and a map of reality that bridges worlds.

In the chapters ahead, we will explore these forms not only as concepts but as **living realities**. You will see how to observe, draw, feel, and work with sacred geometry to bring more beauty, coherence, and awareness into your life.

The patterns are already all around you. This journey will help you begin to **see** them—and perhaps, to see yourself more clearly in the process.

Chapter 3: The Language of Creation — Geometry in Ancient Civilizations

"As above, so below; as within, so without."
— **Hermetic Axiom**

From the soaring pyramids of Egypt to the spiraling temples of the Maya, the sacred geometry embedded in ancient civilizations tells a silent but powerful story. Long before modern science discovered the mathematical codes in nature, ancient cultures across the globe used **geometry as a sacred language**—a tool not just for building structures, but for understanding the cosmos and our place within it.

This chapter takes you on a journey through time, examining how ancient peoples—often without contact or communication with one another—tapped into the same geometric patterns and proportions to **honor the divine**, **align with cosmic forces**, and **encode spiritual knowledge** into their creations.

Why Geometry Was Sacred to the Ancients

To ancient builders, geometry was more than a tool for measurement. It was seen as a mirror of divine order—a **reflection of the cosmos in material form**. Their use of geometry was deeply intentional, aimed at:

- **Aligning structures with celestial bodies**
- **Embodying spiritual principles in physical form**
- **Creating resonance between earth and heaven**
- **Symbolizing universal truths through number and shape**

In sacred geometry, the **temple becomes a model of the universe**, and every stone laid becomes an act of prayer or invocation.

---

1. Egypt: Geometry as Divine Blueprint

Few civilizations used geometry with such monumental precision as the **ancient Egyptians**. The very word "pyramid" is derived from the Greek *pyramis*, which may be linked to *pyra* (fire or light) and *midos* (measure)—hinting at its symbolic and energetic functions.

- The **Great Pyramid of Giza** encodes the **golden ratio (phi)** in the relationship between its base and height.
- Its **orientation is aligned precisely** to true north and the cardinal points.
- The pyramid's dimensions mirror those of the **earth itself**—suggesting a deep understanding of planetary proportions.

The Egyptians believed in **Ma'at**, the principle of cosmic order and balance. Geometry, then, wasn't just mathematics—it was an expression of Ma'at in stone.

Key Symbols:

- The **ankh** – often proportioned geometrically, representing life and the union of opposites
- The **eye of Horus** – encoded with fractions representing divisions of the whole, symbolic of perception and healing
- The **Djed pillar** – a symbol of stability and energetic alignment

2. Mesopotamia: Cosmic Architecture and the Ziggurat

In **Sumer, Babylon, and Assyria**, sacred geometry was woven into the layout of cities, temples, and ziggurats (stepped towers). These cultures were astronomers and mathematicians who mapped the heavens and translated those maps into their sacred buildings.

- The **number 60**, foundational to timekeeping and angular measurement (360 degrees), comes from Sumerian mathematics.
- **Ziggurats** often aligned with planetary cycles and equinox points.
- Temple dimensions reflected **celestial harmonics** and **mythical cosmology**—a multi-leveled universe connected by sacred space.

Sacred Numbers: 7 (planets/layers), 12 (zodiac), 60 (sexagesimal system)

---

3. India: The Geometric Mysticism of the East

In **India**, sacred geometry was a living science—infused into ritual, philosophy, art, and architecture. Temples were constructed based on **vastu shastra**, an ancient system of architectural knowledge rooted in cosmology and geometric grids.

- The **Sri Yantra** is perhaps the most revered symbol in Indian sacred geometry. Composed of **9 interlocking triangles**, it represents the **cosmic womb**—the union of masculine and feminine energies and the structure of the universe.
- **Mandala** means "circle" in Sanskrit and represents a **cosmic diagram**—a visual meditation tool reflecting inner and outer harmony.
- Temples were constructed to mirror the **human energy body (chakra system)** and the journey from material to spiritual.

Key Patterns:

- The **square base and central axis** of Hindu temples mirror the **cosmic axis (Mount Meru)**.

- The **lotus pattern**, seen in architecture and art, reflects the unfolding of consciousness.

---

4. Greece: Geometry as Philosophy and Cosmology

For the **ancient Greeks**, geometry was a divine science—a way of knowing both **the material world and metaphysical truths**. Pythagoras and Plato both emphasized the spiritual power of number and form.

- **Pythagoras** taught that **"all is number"** and discovered musical harmonics through string vibrations—linking math and sound (and thus energy).
- The **Platonic Solids**—five perfectly symmetrical 3D shapes—were associated by Plato with the **elements of nature**: Earth (cube), Air (octahedron), Water (icosahedron), Fire (tetrahedron), and Aether (dodecahedron).
- The **golden ratio** (phi ≈ 1.618) was used in sculpture and architecture, especially the **Parthenon**, symbolizing balance and natural harmony.

For the Greeks, geometry was both a **tool for constructing temples** and a **map for understanding the soul**.

---

5. Mesoamerica: Cosmic Calendars and Geometric Temples

The **Maya, Aztec, and Olmec** civilizations of Central and South America infused their geometry with deep **astronomical insight** and **mythological symbolism**.

- **Pyramids like El Castillo** at Chichén Itzá were aligned with the **equinox sun**, casting a shadow in the form of a serpent descending the stairs.
- The **Mayan calendar system** used precise mathematical cycles based on celestial observations and sacred numbers like 13 and 20.
- Temples and city layouts often reflected **celestial geometry**, including the movements of Venus and the sun.

Geometry was used to **track time, tell myth,** and **connect with the heavens**.

---

6. China: Harmonizing Heaven and Earth

In ancient **China**, sacred geometry was embedded in the principles of **Feng Shui, I Ching**, and the **Taoist understanding of energy**.

- The **Bagua (Pa Kua)** is a geometric octagonal diagram used to map energy flows in space and life, integrating **yin and yang** and the **Five Elements**.
- The **Lo Shu square**, a magic square of numerological importance, was used in designing cities and temples to reflect cosmic harmony.
- **Pagodas**, with their circular and square levels, were built to bridge **earth (square)** and **heaven (circle)**.

Geometry was not seen as abstract but as the **structuring principle of chi**, the life force.

Shared Symbols Across Cultures

Despite vast distances and differences, certain shapes appear **again and again** across ancient civilizations:

- **The circle** – symbol of unity, the infinite, the divine
- **The square** – symbol of matter, the earth, and the human realm
- **The spiral** – evolution, growth, and cosmic energy
- **The triangle** – balance, trinity, and sacred relationships
- **The cross** – intersection of the material and spiritual
- **The labyrinth** – journey to the center of the self

These forms are more than decoration—they were **tools of initiation, maps of the soul**, and **keys to cosmic knowledge**.

Why This Matters Today

Understanding how ancient civilizations used geometry is not just an archaeological curiosity—it's a **wake-up call**. These cultures saw reality as **ordered, meaningful, and interconnected**, and they embedded that worldview into every stone they set and every symbol they carved.

Today, we live in a world often disconnected from the sacred. But the patterns have not disappeared. They are waiting to be seen again—**in nature**, **in your body**, and **in the designs all around you**.

To rediscover sacred geometry is to **reconnect with the wisdom of the ancients**, to reclaim a worldview of beauty, harmony, and wholeness.

Chapter 4: Symbolism and Spirit — Why Shapes Matter

"The soul never thinks without a picture."
— **Aristotle**

What gives a shape its power?

Is a triangle just a triangle? A circle just a circle? Or do these simple forms carry within them something deeper—something spiritual, archetypal, and universal?

In sacred geometry, **shapes are more than visual elements**. They are **living symbols**—bridges between the seen and the unseen, the conscious and the unconscious, the material and the spiritual. Each geometric form expresses a unique **vibrational signature**, a **spiritual principle**, and an **inner truth** that has been recognized by mystics, artists, and sages throughout history.

This chapter explores the **symbolic meaning** behind foundational geometric shapes and how they have been used to convey **cosmic truths**, **psychological insights**, and **spiritual teachings** across cultures and ages.

The Power of Shape as Archetype

In psychology, **Carl Jung** referred to **archetypes** as primordial patterns—universally recognized symbols that arise from the collective unconscious. Sacred geometry deals in similar archetypes, but in visual, mathematical form.

Each shape or pattern carries an **energetic quality**, much like a musical note. These forms resonate with the soul—not because we are taught their meaning, but because we **recognize** it deep within.

We do not need language to understand a spiral's growth, a circle's completeness, or a triangle's balance. These truths are **felt**, not simply analyzed.

Key Shapes and Their Symbolic Meanings

---

1. The Point

Symbol of: Origin, Unity, Divine Potential

The point is the most fundamental concept in geometry. It has no dimension—no height, width, or depth—but it **represents everything**. It is the source of all form.

In sacred symbolism, the point stands for **the One**, the **divine spark**, the **moment of creation**. From the point, all other shapes emerge. It reminds us that behind all multiplicity is **oneness**—formless yet full of infinite potential.

---

2. The Line

Symbol of: Connection, Duality, Path

When the point moves, it becomes a **line**—the first dimension. The line introduces direction, polarity, and **relationship**. It connects two points: **self and other, beginning and end, heaven and earth**.

In spiritual traditions, the line often represents a **path** or **journey**—whether a pilgrimage, a life path, or the movement of energy through space.

---

3. The Circle

Symbol of: Wholeness, Eternity, Unity, The Divine Feminine

The circle is perhaps the most universally sacred shape. With no beginning or end, it represents **infinity, completeness**, and **cosmic unity**. It is the shape of planets, cells, halos, mandalas, and the cycles of life.

Spiritually, the circle is a **container for the sacred**—a boundary that holds, protects, and includes. It is often associated with the **feminine**, the **womb**, and the **divine matrix** from which all forms emerge.

- In **Buddhism**, the **ensō** (Zen circle) symbolizes enlightenment and the void.
- In **Christianity**, the **halo** and **Eucharist** express divine presence.
- In **alchemy**, the circle encloses the **sacred operations** of transformation.

---

4. The Triangle

Symbol of: Balance, Trinity, Transformation, Fire

The triangle introduces **structure and polarity**. With three sides and three points, it is the first shape to enclose space, forming the basis of stability.

Its upward-pointing form symbolizes **aspiration, spirit rising, or fire**, while the downward-pointing triangle represents **water, receptivity, or the divine feminine**.

Spiritually, the triangle is associated with **trinities**:

- **Mind, body, spirit**
- **Past, present, future**
- **Father, Son, Holy Spirit**
- **Creator, preserver, destroyer** (in Hinduism)

The triangle's threefold nature reflects **dynamic balance**—a sacred equilibrium necessary for creation.

5. The Square

Symbol of: Matter, Earth, Foundation, Stability

The square is the archetype of **form**, **material reality**, and **grounding**. With four equal sides and four corners, it represents **stability, logic, and the human-made world**.

In spiritual architecture, temples and altars are often square-based, symbolizing the **foundation of sacred space**. The square relates to the **four elements**, **four directions**, and **four seasons**—markers of earthly existence.

It is the sacred **container of experience**—the place where spirit takes form.

---

6. The Pentagon and Hexagon

Pentagon: Life, the Human Form, Organic Structure
Hexagon: Harmony, Unity in Diversity, Nature's Order

The **pentagon**, with its five sides, is connected to the **human body** (five limbs, five senses) and the **five elements** in many traditions. Its internal star (the pentagram) was sacred to Pythagoreans and symbolized **health, regeneration, and life force**.

The **hexagon**, seen in snowflakes and honeycombs, is nature's most efficient structure. It symbolizes **balance through interconnectedness**. In the **Star of David** and **merkaba**, the hexagram becomes a symbol of **spiritual protection** and **union of opposites**.

---

7. The Spiral

Symbol of: Growth, Expansion, Evolution, Energy Flow

The spiral is one of the oldest and most universal sacred symbols. Found in galaxies, hurricanes, seashells, and ancient carvings, it reflects **dynamic motion**—the path of life unfolding.

It is the **geometry of growth**: from a seed to a flower, from an embryo to a galaxy. Spirals teach us that life moves in **cycles**, but never repeats—each turn brings us to a **new level** of consciousness.

- In **Celtic** and **indigenous** art, spirals symbolize life force and transformation.
- In **kundalini yoga**, the spiral represents the awakening of energy through the spine.

---

8. The Cross

Symbol of: Intersection, Balance, Integration

The cross is the meeting point of **vertical and horizontal, spiritual and material, heaven and earth**. It is a symbol of **sacrifice, union, and integration**.

Before Christianity, the cross was used in many cultures to mark **cosmic alignment, directions**, or the **axis mundi** (world center). It remains a powerful emblem of **equilibrium and centeredness**.

---

9. The Vesica Piscis

Symbol of: Creation, Duality, Portal

Formed by the intersection of two circles, the vesica piscis is a symbol of **birth, union**, and the **interplay of opposites**. It represents the **womb of creation**—where two become one, and one gives birth to many.

This shape appears in Christian iconography (the ichthys or "Jesus fish"), Gothic architecture, and mandorlas around holy figures. It signifies **liminality**—a sacred threshold between worlds.

---

10. The Mandala

Symbol of: Inner Cosmos, Spiritual Order, Meditation

The mandala is a **radial diagram** that combines multiple shapes—circles, squares, triangles—into a visual **map of wholeness**. Used in Eastern and indigenous traditions for meditation and ritual, it symbolizes the **structure of the cosmos and the inner self**.

Each mandala is both a **mirror of the universe** and a **tool for transformation**. By gazing into it or drawing one, you enter a space of **centered awareness**, integrating the fragmented parts of self into unity.

The Emotional and Energetic Impact of Shapes

Why do we feel calm in a circular room, but sharpness in a triangular one? Why do mandalas soothe us, and spirals inspire movement?

Shapes have **energetic signatures**. They affect our nervous system, perception, and emotions. This is why sacred architecture, art, and ritual use geometry so carefully—to **influence states of consciousness**.

- **Circles** induce harmony and openness.
- **Squares** bring stability and order.
- **Spirals** awaken movement and expansion.
- **Triangles** sharpen focus and intention.

By understanding these properties, we can **consciously work with shapes** to align our inner world with outer reality.

Living the Symbols

To engage with sacred geometry is not merely to learn about shapes—it is to **live with them**, to **see through them**, and to **be shaped by them**.

Try this:

- Observe the shapes around you. How do they make you feel?
- Create altars, artwork, or spaces based on geometric intention.
- Meditate on a shape. What insight or energy does it bring?

When you begin to **see the sacred in shape**, everything becomes symbolic. The world becomes a **temple of form**, and every line speaks of spirit.

Shapes matter because they are **blueprints of meaning**. They express eternal truths in visual form and bridge the gap between matter and spirit.

When we learn to speak the language of shape, we begin to **read the world like scripture**—not written in words, but drawn in stars, petals, bones, and breath.

Chapter 5: Number, Frequency, and Form

"If you want to find the secrets of the universe, think in terms of energy, frequency, and vibration."
— **Nikola Tesla**

What if the universe didn't start with a bang—but a **pulse**?

A rhythm.
A vibration.
A tone.

At the deepest level of reality, everything vibrates. Every object, atom, and thought has a **frequency**. And from that frequency, **form arises**. This chapter explores the mystical and mathematical relationship between **number, sound, and shape**—a trinity that lies at the heart of sacred geometry.

Understanding how **number generates frequency**, and how **frequency gives birth to form**, helps us see the world not as static, but as a **living, vibrating web of intelligence**. It reveals why geometry is not just visual—it is **audible, emotional**, and **energetic**.

I. Number: The Code of Creation

In sacred traditions, **numbers are not merely quantities**—they are **qualities**. Each number carries symbolic and vibrational meaning, shaping the geometry and rhythm of the universe. Let's explore the first ten, as they form the foundation of sacred geometry:

1 — Unity

The origin. The singular point. Source energy.
Symbolizes wholeness, divinity, and the monad.

2 — Duality

Polarity, balance, reflection.
Day and night, male and female, yin and yang.

3 — Trinity

Dynamic creation, synthesis of opposites.
Spirit, mind, body. Past, present, future. Birth, life, death.

4 — Stability

The square. Four directions. Four elements.
Earthly foundation.

5 — Life

Human form (five limbs), five senses.
Movement, transformation, health.

6 — Harmony

The hexagon. Star of David.
Balance of opposites within unity.

7 — Spirit

Mysticism, sacred cycles. Seven chakras, seven heavens.
Often linked with spiritual awakening.

8 — Power and Infinity

Balance, cycles, eternity (∞ turned upright).
Material and spiritual mastery.

9 — Completion

The final digit before returning to unity in 10.
Endings, integration, fulfillment.

10 — Return to One

Wholeness and the beginning of a new cycle.
Seen in the Tetractys, a Pythagorean symbol of universal order.

II. Frequency: The Music of Form

Everything in the universe vibrates at a frequency—including shapes. When energy moves through matter, it creates **vibrational patterns**—and when we measure these, we see **form emerging from sound**.

Cymatics: Visual Sound Geometry

In the 20th century, Swiss researcher **Hans Jenny** pioneered the study of **cymatics**—the visible manifestation of sound. By vibrating plates covered in sand or water with pure tones, he revealed complex geometric patterns that form and dissolve depending on the **frequency** used.

- **Low frequencies** create simple shapes (lines, circles).
- **Higher frequencies** generate intricate mandalas, stars, and even **flower-like formations**.

These are not random. The forms correspond to mathematical relationships—particularly the **harmonic ratios** found in music and nature.

Cymatics shows us that **sound is structure**. Frequency is the sculptor of matter.

The Harmonics of the Universe

The universe is not silent—it hums. Planets vibrate. Stars sing. Every object has a **natural frequency** at which it resonates.

In ancient times, temples were built to resonate with certain harmonics. Mantras and chants were designed to stimulate **vibrational centers in the body**. Sound was used not just for communication—but for **transformation**.

Key Harmonic Ratios:

- **Octave (2:1)** – doubling frequency creates a sense of return.
- **Perfect fifth (3:2)** – a powerful stabilizing interval.

- **Golden ratio (~1.618:1)** – found in growth patterns and music, linked to beauty and resonance.

III. Form: Shape Born from Vibration

When frequency becomes visible, it **crystallizes into shape**. This is the transition from energy to matter, from the invisible to the visible.

Let's look at how vibration births form in both nature and geometry.

Fractals and Frequency

Fractals are **self-similar patterns** found in everything from river systems to lungs to lightning. They're created by **repeating simple processes** that expand outward.

- A tree's branches mirror its roots.
- Romanesco broccoli spirals into itself using Fibonacci numbers.
- Snowflakes form crystalline hexagons with infinite variation.

All these forms arise from **vibrational mathematics**—patterns that repeat in space and time, echoing the geometry of sound and number.

Fibonacci and Phi: The Spiral of Life

The **Fibonacci sequence** (1, 1, 2, 3, 5, 8, 13…) describes a growth pattern where each number is the sum of the two before it. As the sequence progresses, the ratio between numbers approaches **Phi (1.618…)**, also known as the **Golden Ratio**.

This ratio appears in:

- Pinecones and sunflower seeds
- DNA spirals
- Spiral galaxies
- Human faces and bodies
- Ancient architecture (like the Parthenon and pyramids)

Phi is **not invented**, but **discovered**—because it is embedded in how energy moves and expands. It is the **mathematical fingerprint of divine proportion**.

Sacred Geometry as Frozen Music

The Greek philosopher **Pythagoras** taught that "geometry is frozen music." What did he mean?

He discovered that musical harmony is based on simple numerical ratios—just like geometric forms. For Pythagoras:

- Music = Number in Time
- Geometry = Number in Space

They are **two aspects of the same truth**: vibrational order. Sacred geometry, then, is music made visible. Mandalas, yantras, and spirals are **songs of form**—frozen echoes of cosmic sound.

IV. The Human Body: A Resonant Form

You are not separate from this pattern. Your body, too, is built on **vibration and proportion**.

- Your DNA coils in a **double spiral**.
- Your bones and organs resonate at specific frequencies.
- Your breath, heart rate, and brain waves form rhythmic cycles.
- Your body follows the **golden ratio**—in your face, limbs, and even the ratio of belly button to height.

Your body is a **musical instrument** and a **sacred geometric temple**. When you chant, sing, dance, or meditate with sacred shapes, you attune yourself to your **true design**.

V. Practical Applications: Using Number and Sound

Sacred geometry is not just to be studied—it's to be **experienced**.

Try These Practices:

1. **Listen to Harmonic Music**: Binaural beats, crystal bowls, or Pythagorean tuning.
2. **Chant Sacred Syllables**: AUM, OM, or seed mantras (bija) that resonate with chakras.
3. **Draw Geometric Patterns**: Begin with the Flower of Life or golden spiral.
4. **Use Numbers in Meditation**: Visualize the qualities of numbers 1 through 9. Let each one guide a different focus (e.g., 4 for grounding, 7 for spirit).
5. **Observe Patterns in Nature**: Look for spirals, symmetry, and proportions wherever you go.

When you see form, ask: **What is the frequency behind this?** When you hear sound, ask: **What form would this create?**

This awareness brings you into **alignment with the living intelligence of the universe**.

- **Number** is not just for counting—it's the archetypal language of the cosmos.
- **Frequency** is the vibrational pulse behind all matter and shape.
- **Form** is the visible crystallization of number and vibration.

Together, they reveal the **divine pattern**—the architecture of energy manifesting in space and time. When we understand this trinity, we begin to experience the universe as a **symphony of shape, sound, and spirit**.

Chapter 6: The Golden Ratio and the Fibonacci Sequence

"There is geometry in the humming of the strings, there is music in the spacing of the spheres."
— **Pythagoras**

Among the many mysteries of sacred geometry, few are as mesmerizing—or as universal—as the **Golden Ratio** and the **Fibonacci Sequence**. Found in the **spiral of galaxies**, the **pattern of petals**, the **growth of seashells**, and even the **human body**, these two mathematical principles are more than just numbers—they are the **blueprint of nature's intelligence**.

In this chapter, we will explore what these patterns are, where they come from, and why they are considered by artists, mystics, and scientists alike to be a key to **cosmic harmony, beauty,** and **universal order**.

I. What Is the Golden Ratio? (Φ)

The **Golden Ratio**, also known by the Greek letter **phi (Φ)**, is an **irrational number** approximately equal to:

Φ ≈ 1.6180339887...

Mathematically, it arises when a line is divided into two parts such that the **whole** is to the **larger part** as the **larger part** is to the **smaller**:

(A + B) / A = A / B = Φ

This simple ratio creates a sense of **proportional perfection**. In geometry, it appears in the **Golden Rectangle**, where the ratio of the sides is φ:1. When you cut a square from this rectangle, the remaining rectangle has the **same proportions**, creating a recursive form that can continue indefinitely.

The Golden Spiral

The **Golden Spiral** is derived from this rectangle: when quarter-circles are drawn within each subdivided section, they form a spiral that **expands while maintaining proportional coherence**.

This spiral appears in:

- **Nautilus shells**
- **Hurricanes**
- **Galaxies**
- **Sunflower seed heads**

- Tornadoes and weather systems

It is nature's way of expanding with **graceful efficiency**.

II. What Is the Fibonacci Sequence?

The **Fibonacci Sequence** is a series of numbers in which each number is the **sum of the two preceding ones**:

0, 1, 1, 2, 3, 5, 8, 13, 21, 34, 55, 89…

This sequence was introduced to the Western world by **Leonardo of Pisa** (aka Fibonacci) in 1202, but it had been known in India and the Middle East centuries earlier.

How It Relates to the Golden Ratio

As the Fibonacci numbers increase, the ratio between each pair of numbers (e.g., 21/13, 34/21, 55/34) approaches the **Golden Ratio**:

$55 \div 34 \approx 1.6176$,
$89 \div 55 \approx 1.6181$

This convergence shows that **Phi is embedded in Fibonacci**, and **Fibonacci is a natural roadmap to Phi**.

III. The Golden Ratio in Nature

Nature doesn't use a calculator, but it follows **Phi** instinctively. The Golden Ratio governs patterns of **growth, efficiency,** and **distribution**. It's how energy naturally flows and organizes itself.

Examples in Nature:

- **Sunflowers**: The seeds spiral outward in both clockwise and counterclockwise directions, often in Fibonacci numbers like 34 and 55.
- **Pinecones & Pineapples**: Display Fibonacci spirals in their segments.

- **Shells**: The nautilus shell grows in a perfect logarithmic spiral approximating the Golden Ratio.
- **Leaves**: Many plants grow leaves in spirals to maximize light exposure, using Fibonacci spacing.
- **DNA**: The structure of the DNA double helix follows the golden ratio in its helical proportions.

This ratio ensures **efficiency, balance,** and **harmony** in organic growth.

IV. The Golden Ratio in the Human Body

Human anatomy is filled with Golden Ratio proportions. This is why classical sculptures and Renaissance portraits—such as those by **Leonardo da Vinci**—are considered **aesthetically perfect**.

Golden Ratio in the Body:

- The ratio of the **forearm to the hand**
- The **distance from navel to floor** vs. **height**
- The **positioning of facial features**
- The **length of the phalanges** in fingers

This has led some to suggest that **the human being is a living expression of sacred proportion.**

V. The Golden Ratio in Art and Architecture

For thousands of years, artists and architects have used the Golden Ratio to create structures and images that **resonate with our innate sense of harmony.**

Examples:

- **The Great Pyramid of Giza**: Its slope approximates the golden ratio.
- **The Parthenon (Greece)**: Proportions match φ in various architectural elements.

- **The Vitruvian Man (da Vinci)**: A study of human symmetry and proportion based on ϕ.
- **The Last Supper**: Structured around Golden Ratio divisions.
- **Modern Logos**: Apple, Twitter, and Pepsi incorporate Golden Ratios in design.

The Golden Ratio is considered **aesthetic** not by accident—but because it **mirrors the order of nature,** and therefore appeals to our deepest visual instincts.

VI. Spiritual and Symbolic Significance

In sacred traditions, the Golden Ratio is more than just pleasing to the eye—it is the **signature of divine order**. It represents:

- **The unfolding of consciousness**
- **The balance of opposites**
- **The infinite within the finite**
- **The process of becoming**

It is a **spiritual metaphor**: life spirals outward, always growing, but always maintaining its connection to origin and essence.

In many mystical systems, Phi is the **geometry of divine evolution**—a perfect balance between chaos and order, complexity and simplicity.

VII. Phi, Fibonacci, and the Universe

The reach of Phi and Fibonacci goes beyond the Earth:

- **Galaxies** spiral in golden proportions.
- **Black holes** form accretion discs with spiral dynamics.
- **Planetary orbits** and the spacing of celestial bodies often reflect harmonic intervals related to Phi.

This suggests that these patterns are not local—but **universal**.

VIII. Experiencing Phi and Fibonacci in Your Life

You don't need to be a mathematician to **feel** the Golden Ratio. You've already experienced it in the flow of time, the curve of your body, and the music that moves you.

Ways to Explore:

- **Draw a Golden Rectangle** and observe its infinite repetition.
- **Use Fibonacci numbers** in creative rhythms or structures (poetry, music, design).
- **Photograph natural objects** and trace their spirals.
- **Design spaces or art** based on Golden Proportions to create harmony.

You can even **meditate on the spiral**, visualizing your breath as an expansion and contraction along its curve—symbolizing the journey between self and cosmos.

- The **Golden Ratio (Φ)** and the **Fibonacci Sequence** are nature's preferred methods of **growth, proportion, and harmony**.
- These patterns appear in **plants, animals, humans, architecture, music, and the cosmos**.
- They are both **scientific truths** and **spiritual metaphors** for life's unfolding intelligence.
- When we work with them—through design, art, contemplation—we bring ourselves into alignment with **universal order**.

Chapter 7: The Platonic Solids – The Building Blocks of Reality

---

"God geometrizes continually."
— **Plato**

For thousands of years, mystics, philosophers, and scientists have contemplated the existence of a divine architecture at the heart of all things. Few geometric forms embody this mystery more powerfully than the **Platonic Solids**. These five perfect, symmetrical three-dimensional shapes are more than mathematical curiosities—they are ancient symbols of the **elements**, **balance**, and **cosmic harmony**.

In this chapter, we will explore:

- What the Platonic Solids are
- Their mathematical and spiritual significance
- Their historical use in sacred traditions
- How they form the hidden scaffolding of the universe

I. What Are the Platonic Solids?

The **Platonic Solids** are the only five three-dimensional shapes in which:

1. All faces are identical regular polygons.
2. All edges are the same length.
3. All angles are the same.
4. The shape fits perfectly inside a sphere.

These five solids are:

Solid	Faces	Element	Symbolism
Tetrahedron	4 triangles	Fire	Willpower, transformation
Cube (Hexahedron)	6 squares	Earth	Stability, physical form
Octahedron	8 triangles	Air	Intellect, breath, balance
Dodecahedron	12 pentagons	Ether (Spirit)	Mystery, cosmos, divine order
Icosahedron	20 triangles	Water	Emotion, intuition, fluidity

These are named after **Plato**, who associated them with the classical elements in his dialogue **Timaeus**, written around 360 BCE.

II. The Geometry of Perfection

Mathematical Elegance

Each Platonic Solid is a **model of perfect balance**—symmetrical in every direction. They demonstrate:

- **Equidistant vertices** (all corners touch the surface of a surrounding sphere)
- **Equal edges and angles**
- **Duality**: Each solid has a **dual**—another Platonic Solid that results when the centers of the faces are connected.

Solid	Dual
Tetrahedron	Tetrahedron
Cube	Octahedron
Octahedron	Cube
Dodecahedron	Icosahedron
Icosahedron	Dodecahedron

This duality reflects a cosmic principle: **everything has a mirror**, and harmony comes from understanding the interplay between opposites.

III. The Solids and the Elements

Plato believed the physical world was composed of combinations of the five elements, each represented by a Platonic Solid. Here's how the geometry corresponds to each:

Tetrahedron – Fire

- Sharp points and edges suggest **energy, transformation**, and motion.
- Represents **will, power**, and **spiritual awakening**.
- Balances action and purification.

Cube (Hexahedron) – Earth

- Square faces and a grounded shape convey **solidity, structure**, and **support**.
- Symbolizes **foundation, material reality**, and the **physical body**.

Octahedron – Air

- Light, expansive structure with points facing above and below.
- Encourages **mental clarity, communication**, and **breath**.
- Used in meditative balance and heart-based awareness.

Icosahedron – Water

- Many triangular faces create a flowing, almost spherical form.
- Symbolizes **emotion, intuition**, and the subconscious.
- Inspires adaptability and inner movement.

Dodecahedron – Ether/Spirit

- The most mysterious, with twelve pentagonal faces.
- Ancient symbol of the **cosmos, heaven**, and the **infinite**.
- Thought to represent the **unmanifest**, the **divine**, and the **akashic field**.

In many esoteric traditions, the **dodecahedron** is seen as the shape of the **universe itself**, holding within it the secret of multidimensional reality.

IV. The Solids in Ancient Cultures

Pythagoras and the Mystery Schools

Though credited to Plato, the solids were likely known to **Pythagorean schools** and earlier traditions. Pythagoras taught that all matter was composed of vibrating geometries. For him, geometry was the language of the divine.

Sacred Use in Ancient Cultures:

- **Ancient Egypt**: Pyramid geometry mirrors tetrahedral energy.

- **Greece**: Temples were built using cube-based structures for stability and balance.
- **India & Tibet**: Mandalas and yantras include nested three-dimensional forms resembling Platonic solids.
- **Celtic & Druidic traditions**: Used dodecahedral stones for rituals.
- **Native American traditions**: Employed sacred geometry in medicine wheels and architecture.

The Platonic Solids were **not just studied—they were revered**. They symbolized the **architecture of the soul**.

V. Hidden in Nature and the Cosmos

Despite their abstract appearance, Platonic Solids appear frequently in the **natural world**:

Examples in Nature:

- **Carbon molecules** (like Buckminsterfullerene or "Buckyballs") are shaped like truncated icosahedrons.
- **Viruses** often have **icosahedral** protein shells.
- **Crystal structures** often mirror cube or tetrahedral forms.
- **Snowflakes** form from **octahedral lattice structures**.
- **DNA molecules** are stabilized by tetrahedral bonds.

Even **space-time itself**, according to some physicists, may be structured by geometric fields and vibrations that mirror the solids.

VI. The Platonic Solids in Metaphysics

In metaphysical terms, the solids are seen as:

- **Energy containers** for the elemental forces
- **Templates** for chakras, auras, and subtle bodies
- **Meditation aids** to align consciousness with universal order

Chakra Connections (as used by some healers):

- **Tetrahedron (Fire)** – Solar Plexus Chakra
- **Cube (Earth)** – Root Chakra
- **Octahedron (Air)** – Heart Chakra
- **Icosahedron (Water)** – Sacral Chakra
- **Dodecahedron (Spirit)** – Crown Chakra

Working with these shapes energetically can **restore balance**, enhance **clarity**, and deepen **spiritual perception**.

VII. Using the Solids in Practice

Here are some ways readers can **experience** the power of these shapes directly:

1. Meditation with Shapes

Hold or visualize a solid during meditation. Allow it to align your mind and body with its elemental energy.

2. Crystal Grids

Use stones carved in these shapes to enhance energy fields in your space. Each solid amplifies the qualities of its associated element.

3. Drawing or Modeling

Draw the nets (flat shapes) of the solids and fold them into 3D models. This tactile creation connects the hands and mind with sacred proportions.

4. Visualization for Healing

Visualize each solid spinning within the corresponding chakra to clear, energize, and align your subtle energy system.

VIII. The Solids and the Flower of Life

A fascinating discovery emerges when you extend the **Flower of Life** into three dimensions. Within it, you can derive:

- All five Platonic Solids
- Metatron's Cube
- The Merkaba (light body vehicle)
- The structure of atoms and molecular bonding

This shows that these shapes are not separate from sacred symbols—they are **encoded within the very patterns of universal creation**.

- The **Platonic Solids** are five perfect three-dimensional forms that reflect the underlying architecture of the universe.
- They represent the **five classical elements**—earth, air, fire, water, and spirit.
- These shapes appear in **nature**, **mysticism**, **art**, and **science**, from crystal structures to cosmic patterns.
- By understanding and working with them, we begin to align with the **geometry of balance, harmony, and transcendence**.

These shapes are more than forms—they are **gateways**. In the next chapter, we will explore the **circle**, the most ancient and sacred of all shapes, and how it represents **unity, infinity, and the source of all creation**.

Chapter 8: The Power of the Point, Line, and Circle

"All things begin with a point, extend as a line, and come into wholeness as a circle."
— Ancient Hermetic Teaching

Before the complexity of Platonic solids, spirals, or mandalas, sacred geometry begins with **three primal forms**: the **point**, the **line**, and the **circle**. These are not only basic elements of geometry but also **symbolic archetypes** of **creation**, **existence**, and **consciousness**. They form the **alphabet** from which all sacred geometry—and, indeed, all form—arises.

This chapter explores:

- The symbolic and metaphysical significance of the point, line, and circle
- How they appear in sacred traditions, nature, and consciousness
- Their role as the foundations of sacred geometry

I. The Point: The Seed of Creation

Definition

In geometry, a **point** is defined as a location with no dimension—no length, width, or depth. It is pure **position** without form.

Symbolic Meaning

- **The beginning of all things**
- **Unity**, **origin**, or the **divine spark**
- Represents the **Source**—God, the Tao, the Absolute

In many spiritual traditions, the point is **the unmanifest potential**. It is the **dot at the center** of the circle, the **stillness** from which movement arises.

The Monad

In Pythagorean philosophy, the point corresponds to the **Monad**, the first principle. It is **undivided unity**, from which duality and multiplicity emerge.

II. The Line: The Path of Creation

Definition

A **line** is formed by connecting two points. It has **one dimension**—length—but no width or height.

Symbolic Meaning

- **Connection, duality**, and **direction**
- The journey from the **infinite potential** (point) into **manifest reality**
- Often seen as the **ray of creation** or **consciousness in motion**

In esoteric teachings, the line represents the **first movement of consciousness**—the beam of light emerging from the void, the path of the soul, or the axis mundi connecting heaven and earth.

The Dyad

The line corresponds to the **Dyad** in Pythagorean terms: the first relationship, or the awareness of "other." It introduces **polarity**—light/dark, self/other, spirit/matter.

III. The Circle: Wholeness and the Womb of Creation

Definition

A **circle** is a continuous curve in which all points are equidistant from a central point. It is the **first two-dimensional shape** and symbolizes **infinity** and **perfection**.

Symbolic Meaning

- **Totality, infinity, cycles, eternity**
- The **womb of creation** and the **sacred feminine**
- The **boundary of existence**—holding and containing space

The circle is one of the most **universal sacred symbols**, found across cultures and eras. It is the **halo**, the **wheel of time**, the **sun**, the **cell**, and the **cosmic egg**.

The Vesica Piscis and Flower of Life

By overlapping circles (starting with two), the **Vesica Piscis** and **Flower of Life** emerge—foundational symbols in sacred geometry. Thus, the circle isn't just wholeness; it's also a **portal to complexity**.

IV. The Geometry of Creation: From Point to Universe

1. **Point (Monad)** – Absolute Unity
   → Divine potential, the seed of creation

2. **Line (Dyad)** – Conscious Division
   → First movement, duality, awareness of opposites

3. **Circle (Triad)** – Contained Space
   → First shape, feminine container, wholeness, time

This movement—from **singularity to multiplicity**, from **nothing to something**—is the **story of creation** encoded in geometry. Each step is both **literal** and **symbolic**.

V. Sacred Traditions and the Primordial Forms

Egyptian and Hermetic Thought

- The **point** was called the "hidden spark" or **Atum**, the undivided.
- The **line** was the extension of divine will.
- The **circle** was the **Ouroboros** (serpent eating its tail), symbolizing eternity.

Kabbalah

- The **point** is **Ein Sof**, the infinite divine light.
- The **line** becomes the **Kav**, the ray of creation.
- The **circle** is the **Olam**, the created world, the container of divine attributes.

Eastern Mysticism

- In **Tantra**, the **bindu** (point) is the source of all manifestation.
- The **circle** forms **mandalas**, sacred maps of consciousness.
- The **line** is the **nadi**, or energetic pathway.

Native Traditions

- The **medicine wheel** is a sacred circle of time, space, and direction.
- The **path** between worlds is marked by straight lines connecting sacred points.
- **Circle dances** reflect spiritual unity and natural cycles.

VI. The Point, Line, and Circle in Nature

- **Point**: The **nucleus** of an atom, the **center** of a flower, the **eye** of a storm.
- **Line**: **Tree trunks, rivers, lightning bolts,** or **the horizon**.
- **Circle**: The **orbit** of planets, the **cell membrane**, the **sun, ripples on water**.

These primal forms appear not just in concept, but in **living reality**—shaping the world around us and within us.

VII. Psychological and Spiritual Dimensions

- The **point** is the **self before differentiation**, pure awareness.
- The **line** represents the **ego's journey**, choice, and purpose.
- The **circle** is the **whole psyche**, the **Self** (in Jungian terms), where all aspects are integrated.

Carl Jung saw the **mandala** (a circle with a center) as a representation of the **individuation process**—the journey toward spiritual wholeness.

VIII. Practical Exercises and Meditations

1. The Dot Meditation (The Point)

- Gaze at a small black dot on white paper.
- Let it symbolize infinite potential, emptiness, or your essence.
- Ask: *What wants to emerge from this stillness?*

2. The Line Drawing Exercise

- Draw a single, straight line.
- Reflect on direction, polarity, and the path between two truths.
- Ask: *What lies at the midpoint between opposites in my life?*

3. The Circle Walking Ritual

- Create a circle with stones or rope.
- Walk its perimeter slowly, meditating on containment and continuity.

- Step into the center to symbolically enter unity and the heart of creation.

IX. Summary: The Sacred Trinity of Form

Form	Dimension	Symbolism	Spiritual Meaning
Point	0D	Origin, seed, divinity	Pure potential, divine spark
Line	1D	Journey, polarity	Conscious movement, duality
Circle	2D	Wholeness, eternity	Completion, sacred feminine, unity

These three primal forms form the **trinity of manifestation**. Everything in sacred geometry—and in creation—unfolds from their dynamic interplay. To understand them is to begin speaking the **language of the universe**.

From the infinite perfection of the circle, geometry evolves into increasingly complex yet harmonious patterns. In the next chapter, we will explore the **symbolism and meaning of the triangle**—the first true polygon, the **number three**, and the sacred balance of opposites and unity.

Part II: Sacred Shapes and Their Meanings

Chapter 9: The Circle — Unity, Wholeness, and Infinity

"The circle is the shape of the divine: without beginning, without end."
— Ancient Hermetic Proverb

The **circle** is the most ancient and universal of all geometric forms. It is found in the sun and the moon, the ripples in a pond, the iris of the eye, and the orbit of planets. Revered across cultures and traditions, the circle represents **unity, completion, perfection**, and **the infinite**.

In sacred geometry, the circle is not merely a shape—it is the **template of all creation**. Everything that exists begins in a circle and unfolds from it.

I. The Geometry of the Circle

- **Mathematically**, a circle is defined as the set of all points equidistant from a center point.
- It has **no edges, corners, or direction**—it is continuous, closed, and balanced in every possible orientation.
- Its key measurements—**radius, diameter, and circumference**—form the basis of advanced sacred geometry when connected with ratios like **π (pi)** and the **Golden Ratio**.

II. Symbolic Meaning of the Circle

The circle carries profound metaphysical and spiritual meanings across time and tradition:

Symbolic Aspect	Meaning
Unity	The One, Oneness with Source
Wholeness	Integrity, completeness, totality
Infinity	Timelessness, the eternal cycle
The Divine Feminine	Womb of creation, receptivity, containment
Perfection	Balance, symmetry, harmony
Cycles	Life, death, rebirth; the wheel of time

The circle **contains**. It **protects**. It **connects** all within its perimeter, yet **excludes nothing**. It is both the container and the contained.

III. The Circle in Nature and the Cosmos

Nature expresses the circle with astonishing consistency. It is the preferred form in environments where **balance, energy efficiency, and harmony** are required.

Natural Expressions of the Circle:

- **Celestial bodies**: The sun, moon, and planets are spherical, their orbits forming circular or elliptical paths.
- **Cells**: The first form of life begins as a **circular cell**, the biological foundation of all living things.
- **Ripples**: When a drop hits water, it sends out **concentric circles**, echoing the spread of energy.
- **Tree rings**: Circles within the trunk show the **passage of time and growth**.
- **Flowers**: Many flowers, such as daisies or sunflowers, form petals around a central point in **circular symmetry**.

Nature favors the circle because it represents **efficiency and flow**. It minimizes surface tension and distributes energy evenly.

IV. The Sacred Circle Across Cultures

Throughout human history, the circle has been used to represent the **sacred**, the **eternal**, and the **cosmic order**.

1. Mandalas (Tibet, India)

- Mandalas are circular designs that represent **spiritual wholeness** and **the universe**.
- Used as **meditation tools**, they symbolize the inner journey toward the divine center.

2. The Medicine Wheel (Native American)

- A sacred circle representing the **four directions, seasons**, and **cycles of life**.
- Used in healing rituals, vision quests, and teachings about **balance and harmony**.

3. Ouroboros (Egypt, Greece)
- A **snake eating its tail**, forming a circle.
- Symbol of **eternal return**, **infinity**, and **regeneration**.

4. The Enso (Zen Buddhism)
- A hand-drawn circle representing **enlightenment**, **emptiness**, and **the perfection of imperfection**.
- Created in a single breath, it reflects the **present moment**.

5. Stone Circles (Celtic, Neolithic Europe)
- Structures like **Stonehenge** are built in circular formations, aligned to celestial cycles.
- Served as **calendars**, **ritual spaces**, and **portals to the divine**.

The recurring use of the circle suggests an **intuitive recognition** of its symbolic and energetic power.

V. The Circle as Womb and Portal

The circle is often associated with the **feminine principle**—it **contains** and **nurtures**. It is:

- The **womb** from which all creation emerges.
- The **portal** between worlds—birth and death, spirit and matter.
- The **cosmic egg**, found in myths of creation from India, Egypt, Greece, and beyond.

In this way, the circle becomes more than a shape; it becomes the **matrix of manifestation**, a **vessel of divine potential**.

VI. The Circle and Time

The circle teaches us that time is not linear—it is **cyclical**.

- **The seasons** repeat in circular rhythm: spring → summer → autumn → winter → spring.

- **Day and night** rotate continuously.
- The **zodiac**, **lunar cycles**, and **planetary orbits** are all circular.

Ancient peoples lived by the circle. Their calendars, agricultural practices, and festivals were governed by **sacred time**, not linear progress. They saw existence as **ever-returning**, not ever-ending.

VII. Spiritual Practices with the Circle

1. Meditation: Entering the Circle

- Visualize a radiant circle of light surrounding you.
- Step into it mindfully and let it hold you in wholeness.
- Feel your connection to all things—centered, safe, and eternal.

2. Drawing Sacred Circles

- Create your own **mandala**, beginning with a circle.
- Allow symbols, colors, and patterns to emerge intuitively.
- Let the act of drawing become a form of prayer or insight.

3. Circle Walking

- Walk slowly in a large circle (indoors or outside).
- Reflect on cycles in your own life: what's ending, what's beginning?
- Use each step as an intention to **reclaim your wholeness**.

4. Build a Circle Altar

- Arrange candles, stones, or flowers in a circle.
- Place something sacred at the center.
- Use it as a space for quiet reflection or ritual.

VIII. The Circle and Sacred Geometry Patterns

The circle is the **template** upon which almost all sacred geometric figures are built. For example:

- **The Vesica Piscis**: Two intersecting circles create a lens shape—the seed of all further forms.
- **The Seed of Life**: Seven overlapping circles forming a flower-like pattern.
- **The Flower of Life**: A vast lattice of circles containing the blueprint of creation.
- **Metatron's Cube**: Derivable from a circle-based grid, containing all Platonic solids.

These forms all begin with **circles arranged around a central point**, demonstrating that the circle is not only the **origin**, but also the **path to complexity** and **interconnection**.

IX. Summary: The Wisdom of the Circle

Circle Symbolism	Meaning
Center Point	Divine origin, source, stillness
Outer Edge	Boundary of being, containment
Unbroken Line	Eternity, continuity, timelessness
Inner Space	Sacred womb, potential, creation
Motion Around Center	Balance, cycles, rhythm of life

To engage with the circle is to engage with **unity, wholeness**, and the **cosmic intelligence** that binds all things. It is the **first sacred space**, both simple and infinitely deep.

Chapter 10: The Triangle — The Divine Trinity

"The triangle is the first form to emerge from unity and duality—a symbol of divine balance, spiritual ascent, and cosmic order."

The triangle is the **first polygon**, the simplest closed shape that introduces **sides, angles**, and **structure** to geometry. As the third stage in the progression from **point** to **line** to **circle**, the triangle embodies the principle of **three**—the number of **manifestation, balance,** and **wholeness-in-motion.**

Revered in mysticism, religion, and architecture, the triangle is known as a symbol of the **divine trinity,** and is often used to represent **ascent, integration,** and the **dynamic balance of opposites.**

I. The Geometry of the Triangle

- A **triangle** is a closed, two-dimensional figure with **three sides** and **three angles**.
- The sum of its internal angles always equals **180°**.
- The triangle introduces **directionality** and **stability** to form.

Types of Triangles

- **Equilateral** (all sides and angles equal): Harmony, perfection, spiritual balance.
- **Isosceles** (two sides equal): Balance of duality and singularity.
- **Scalene** (no sides equal): Diversity within structure.
- **Right-angled triangle**: Foundation of Pythagorean and architectural principles.

II. The Spiritual Symbolism of the Number Three

In **numerology** and **sacred traditions, three** is the number of:

- **Creation** (1+2=3: unity and duality give birth to form)
- **Balance** (between extremes)
- **Trinity** (unifying opposites with a higher third)

Examples of Divine Trinities

Tradition	Trinity Elements
Christianity	Father, Son, Holy Spirit

Tradition	Trinity Elements
Hinduism	Brahma, Vishnu, Shiva
Ancient Egypt	Osiris, Isis, Horus
Kabbalah	Keter, Chokmah, Binah
Alchemy	Sulfur, Mercury, Salt
Mind/Body/Spirit	Unity of human experience

The triangle often **embodies these trinities**, visually and symbolically.

III. The Triangle as a Spiritual Map

1. The Base and the Apex

- The **base** represents the physical world—**duality**, stability, material foundation.
- The **apex** points to the spiritual realm—**oneness**, transcendence, divine purpose.

Thus, the triangle becomes a **map of ascent**—moving from earthly duality to spiritual unity.

2. The Dynamic Between Opposites

- Two lower points represent **opposing forces** (light/dark, male/female, inner/outer).
- The top point represents **integration**—transcending polarity through consciousness.

This expresses a central teaching of sacred geometry: **true harmony is not found in eliminating difference, but in unifying it at a higher level.**

IV. The Triangle in Ancient Cultures and Esoteric Systems

1. The Pythagoreans

- The **tetractys**, a triangular arrangement of ten points, represented **cosmic harmony** and the structure of the universe.

- The triangle was considered the form of **fire**, representing **transformation** and **divine energy**.

2. The Greeks and the Golden Triangle

- The **isosceles triangle** with two 72° angles and one 36° angle was revered for its connection to the **Golden Ratio**.
- Used in architecture, art, and mystery schools as a symbol of **divine proportion**.

3. Alchemy

- Triangles were used to symbolize the **four elements**:
    - ▲ Upward triangle: **Fire**
    - ▽ Downward triangle: **Water**
    - ▲ with a line: **Air**
    - ▽ with a line: **Earth**
- Also used to express the union of **masculine** (upward triangle) and **feminine** (downward triangle) energies.

4. The Sri Yantra

- In Hindu sacred geometry, nine interlocking triangles form the **Sri Yantra**, symbolizing the cosmos and the union of Shiva and Shakti.

V. The Triangle and the Human Experience

1. Mind–Body–Spirit

The triangle can represent the integration of all aspects of self:

- **Mind**: Thought, reason, logic
- **Body**: Form, action, presence
- **Spirit**: Intuition, purpose, divine connection

Together, they create a balanced human being.

2. Past–Present–Future

Time itself is triadic. Awareness of the triangle teaches us that we are not linear beings—we exist in **cyclical patterns** that fold into themselves.

3. Observer–Observed–Observation

In quantum theory and mysticism alike, reality arises not from separate components, but from the **relationship between three**.

VI. The Triangle in Sacred Architecture and Art

- **Pyramids** (Egypt, Mesoamerica): 3D triangles designed to **amplify energy**, represent ascent, and align with celestial bodies.
- **Gothic cathedrals**: Incorporate triangular shapes in **arches**, **vaults**, and **window design**, symbolizing divine light and order.
- **Christian art**: Triangles used to depict the **Trinity**, halos, and divine geometry.
- **Tibetan mandalas**: Use of interlocking triangles to represent **masculine and feminine forces** in union.

The triangle is more than symbolic—it is **functional**, shaping energy, space, and consciousness.

VII. Triangles and Energy Flow

Triangles are used in **energy healing**, **architecture**, and **ritual** because:

- They direct **upward or downward motion** of spiritual energy.
- Pointing **up**, they activate **higher chakras, ascension**, and **masculine energy**.
- Pointing **down**, they ground energy into the earth, invoke **feminine energy**, and deepen **receptivity**.

Combined together (such as in the **Star of David** or **Merkaba**), upward and downward triangles represent the **harmonious union** of heaven and earth.

VIII. Meditations and Practices with the Triangle

1. Triangle Breathing

- Inhale (count of 4), hold (count of 4), exhale (count of 4).
- Visualize each breath forming one side of a glowing triangle around your body.

2. Drawing the Sacred Triangle

- Draw a triangle on paper.
- Assign personal meanings to each point (e.g., mind/body/spirit).
- Journal about how these three aspects interact in your life.

3. Build a Triangle Altar

- Place three candles or stones at the corners of a triangle.
- Sit in the center and meditate on unity and integration.

4. Triangle Walking (Trikona Kriya)

- Walk in a triangular path (e.g., 3x3 meters).
- With each corner, pause and reflect on one aspect of a triad (e.g., past, present, future).

IX. Summary: The Sacred Meaning of the Triangle

Aspect	Symbolism
Three Points	Manifestation, completion, balance
Base	Duality, foundation, physical reality
Apex	Unity, spirit, divine ascent
Shape	Fire, direction, energy, motion
Function	Connector between heaven and earth

The triangle is a **gateway to structure, creation, and spiritual insight**. It reveals that **truth often lies not in opposition, but in the higher synthesis of opposites**. In sacred geometry, the triangle marks the **first moment of form**, of becoming, of divine manifestation in space.

Chapter 11: The Square — Earth, Stability, and Manifestation

"The square is the foundation stone of the material world. It brings order to chaos, gives boundaries to energy, and reveals the sacredness of the physical realm."

In the journey of sacred geometry, the **square** represents a moment of grounding. After the generative unity of the **circle**, the ascent of the **triangle**, and the spiritual integration they bring, the square brings energy **down to Earth**. It is the **geometry of the material world**, the symbol of **structure, containment, and stability**.

This chapter explores the square as a sacred form deeply connected to the **four elements, four directions**, and the **material plane**, showing how it serves as a framework through which **spirit manifests as matter**.

I. The Geometry of the Square

- A **square** is a four-sided polygon with equal-length sides and four 90° angles.
- It is the simplest **regular quadrilateral**, offering perfect **symmetry** and **balance**.
- It provides **containment**, acting as a stable container for energy, intention, or design.

The square's geometry is both **precise** and **practical**, forming the foundation of temples, cities, homes, and altars across cultures.

II. Symbolic Meaning of the Square

Symbolic Aspect	Meaning
Earth	Materiality, grounding, stability
Structure	Order, law, foundation
The Number Four	Balance, manifestation, integration of spirit

Symbolic Aspect **Meaning**

Matter and Form The visible, tangible realm

Sacred Space The altar, temple, or sacred enclosure

Where the **triangle** seeks the heavens, the **square** holds the world in place.

III. The Number Four and the Physical World

In sacred numerology, **four** is the number of the **material universe**. It represents the **completion of form** and the **stabilization** of energy in the physical world.

Symbolic Representations of Four:

- **Four elements**: Earth, Air, Fire, Water
- **Four directions**: North, South, East, West
- **Four seasons**: Spring, Summer, Autumn, Winter
- **Four limbs / four corners**: Human structure and sacred space
- **Four phases of the moon**: New, Waxing, Full, Waning

This recurrence is no coincidence—it reveals that four is the number through which **spirit becomes structure**.

IV. The Square in Ancient Cultures

1. Egypt: The Square in Temple Design

- Egyptian temples were based on **sacred grids** formed by squares.
- These reflected the cosmic order, mirroring the heavens on Earth.
- The square was also associated with **Maat**, the goddess of truth and balance.

2. China: Earth as the Square

- In Chinese cosmology, **Earth was square**, and **Heaven was round**.

- The **Lo Shu Square**, a 3x3 magic square, represented cosmic order and balance.
- Temples and cities were laid out in **square grids**, aligning with **geomantic principles** (feng shui).

3. Native Traditions: The Medicine Wheel

- Though circular in form, the medicine wheel is often divided into **four quadrants**, each representing a direction, an element, and an aspect of life.
- The **sacred lodge** or ceremonial grounds are often built on a square base, grounding spiritual ritual in form.

4. Freemasonry and the Square

- The **Masonic square** represents morality, structure, and the alignment of personal life with cosmic order.
- "Squaring your actions" means living in truth and balance.

V. The Square in Sacred Architecture

Throughout the world, **sacred structures** begin with the square as their **foundation**:

- **Temples**: From the Hindu mandir to the Jewish Tabernacle, squares are used as the base form.
- **Pyramids**: The Great Pyramid has a perfect square base aligned to the cardinal directions.
- **Cathedrals**: Many are designed using square floor plans, overlaid with sacred proportions.
- **Altars**: Typically square or rectangular, symbolizing a stable container for divine energy.

The square is not merely architectural—it is **spirit crystallized into space**.

VI. The Square and the Human Body

The **Vitruvian Man** by Leonardo da Vinci demonstrates that the human form fits both a **circle** and a **square**, symbolizing the dual nature of humanity:

- The **circle**: Our divine, spiritual potential
- The **square**: Our grounded, earthly embodiment

To live well is to balance both—the infinite with the practical, the eternal with the present moment.

VII. The Square as a Spiritual Tool

Because of its **balance and containment**, the square is ideal for creating sacred space.

1. Square Mandalas

- In Eastern traditions, mandalas often use **nested squares** to represent the journey from external form to inner essence.
- Each layer of the square acts as a **threshold**, a passage inward.

2. Grids and Altars

- Sacred grids (like the **crystal grid**) are arranged on square patterns to create focused energetic fields.
- An altar built on a square cloth can represent the **four elements**, the **four directions**, or the **four intentions** of a ritual.

3. Grounding Meditation

- Sit inside a square marked by four stones or candles.
- Visualize each corner representing one of the four elements.
- Feel your body drawing strength from this balanced base.

VIII. The Square and the Cube: 3D Manifestation

In three dimensions, the square becomes the **cube**, the geometric embodiment of material solidity and spatial order.

Cube Symbolism:

- **Earth element** in Platonic Solids
- Represents **stability, permanence, and groundedness**
- Used in **sacred geometry** to represent the **physical realm**

The cube's six faces and twelve edges represent multidimensional balance—perfect for understanding matter as a **vessel for divine order**.

IX. Sacred Geometry Patterns Emerging from Squares

- **The Grid**: A square-based lattice upon which complex patterns are built.
- **The Flower of Life** can be laid out on a square grid for structural precision.
- **Vesica Piscis arrangements** can be squared off to form crystalline structures.
- The **Metatron's Cube**, though circular in presentation, hides square relationships in its geometric base.

The **square is both blueprint and boundary**—it allows divine inspiration to be carried into form.

X. Summary: The Sacred Function of the Square

Square Element Symbolic Function

Square Element	Symbolic Function
Four Sides	Stability, completeness, containment
Right Angles	Order, symmetry, grounded structure
Alignment	Relationship to the four directions/elements
Square Base	Foundation for sacred space and creation
Cube	3D manifestation of matter and consciousness

In sacred geometry, the square teaches us how to **bring spirit into matter**, how to **manifest potential into form**, and how to **live in alignment** with the deep structures of the universe.

Chapter 12: The Pentagon and Hexagon — Natural Harmony

"The pentagon and hexagon reveal the elegance of nature's intelligence, where growth and balance converge in sacred design."

As we journey through sacred geometry, we now reach two interrelated forms that reflect nature's **harmonious intelligence**: the **pentagon** (five-sided shape) and the **hexagon** (six-sided shape). Unlike the square, which anchors and defines, these geometries introduce **organic flow, growth, and interconnection**.

Both shapes appear frequently in natural systems, from **honeycombs and crystals** to **flowers and shells**. They hold profound symbolic and mathematical meaning, expressing **life, beauty, proportion, and interconnectedness**.

I. The Pentagon: The Symbol of Life and Regeneration

What Is a Pentagon?

- A **pentagon** is a five-sided polygon with internal angles summing to 540°.
- A **regular pentagon** has five equal sides and angles.
- When inscribed in a circle, it produces the **five-pointed star** or **pentagram**.

Symbolism of Five

- **Five elements** in many systems (earth, water, fire, air, and ether/spirit)
- **Five fingers, five toes, five senses** — deeply human number
- In numerology, five represents **change, adaptability, and life force**

The Pentagram and the Golden Ratio

- The **pentagram**, drawn within a pentagon, reveals **golden ratio (φ)** relationships between its segments.
- The golden ratio is found in:

- The human body (e.g., limb proportions)
- DNA spirals
- Flower petal arrangements

This makes the pentagram a **map of organic growth** and a **symbol of divine proportion**.

Ancient and Esoteric Use

- **Pythagoreans** revered the pentagram as a symbol of health and harmony.
- **Wiccans** and modern mystics use it to represent **balance among the elements**, with the top point representing **spirit**.
- In **alchemy**, it signifies the **union of opposites** to create a living whole.

II. The Pentagon in Nature and the Human Body

- Many flowers (e.g., morning glory, wild rose) have **five petals**, arranged in pentagonal symmetry.
- **Starfish** exhibit natural pentagonal structure.
- The human body mirrors the **pentagram**:
    - Head, arms, and legs form a five-pointed star
    - Ratios between navel, head, and limbs reflect φ

Thus, the pentagon/pentagram is not just a concept — it is a **blueprint of life**.

III. The Hexagon: Nature's Efficient Pattern

What Is a Hexagon?

- A **hexagon** is a six-sided polygon with internal angles totaling 720°.
- A **regular hexagon** can be perfectly divided into six **equilateral triangles**.

- It tiles a plane **without gaps**, making it extremely **efficient** for packing and space.

Symbolism of Six

- **Six directions**: up, down, left, right, forward, back — totality of space
- **Balance between polarities**: male/female, spirit/matter
- In numerology, six represents **harmony, family, and integration**

Hexagons in Nature

- **Beehives**: Hexagons use the least material to store the most honey
- **Snowflakes**: Water molecules freeze into hexagonal crystalline structures
- **Turtle shells, carbon structures** (graphene), **flower centers** — all use hexagonal symmetry

The hexagon is nature's choice for **efficiency, strength, and symmetry**.

IV. The Star of David and the Merkabah

- The **Star of David** is made of two overlapping **equilateral triangles**, forming a **six-pointed star** — a sacred hexagonal symbol.
- Represents:
    - Union of opposites (heaven/earth, male/female)
    - Interdimensional geometry (used in **Merkabah meditation**)
- Often placed inside a **hexagon**, it becomes a symbol of **balance between worlds**.

V. Comparing the Pentagon and Hexagon

Aspect	Pentagon	Hexagon
Sides	5	6

Aspect	Pentagon	Hexagon
Symbolic Number	Life, growth, transformation	Harmony, structure, unity in space
Shape in Nature	Flowers, starfish, human body	Honeycomb, crystals, snowflakes
Inner Geometry	Pentagram (golden ratio)	Triangles (equilateral tiling)
Esoteric Meaning	Life force, sacred feminine, spirit	Totality, divine union, cosmic harmony

Each shape carries a unique energetic quality:

- **The pentagon** is alive, regenerative, expressive.
- **The hexagon** is integrative, grounding, cosmic.

VI. Sacred Geometry in Action: Using Pentagons and Hexagons

1. Meditation with Geometric Visuals

- Visualize a **pentagram** glowing from your heart outward, representing your vitality.
- Meditate within a **hexagonal mandala** for grounding and connection to universal harmony.

2. Drawing and Mapping

- Practice constructing a **perfect pentagon** and inscribing the **golden spiral**.
- Draw **hexagonal grids**, connecting them into flower-like forms (like the **Seed of Life**).

3. Ritual Tools and Altars

- Use five or six objects placed in a pentagonal or hexagonal layout to enhance energy flow.
- Create a **five-element altar** using a pentagram orientation for balance.

VII. The Deeper Meaning: Growth Through Pattern

Both the pentagon and hexagon teach us how **patterns guide life**:

- The **pentagon** reminds us that life is not static; it **spirals and evolves**.
- The **hexagon** reveals that connection and harmony are achieved through **structure and unity**.

In combining growth and balance, these shapes reflect the **cosmic intelligence embedded in nature**.

VIII. Summary: Nature's Divine Patterns

Shape	Essence	Sacred Message
Pentagon	Life, growth, golden proportion	Life is dynamic, harmonious, and divinely ordered
Hexagon	Structure, balance, interconnection	Unity and order are at the heart of the universe

Sacred geometry invites us to **see the world as a symphony of shapes**, each playing a role in the grand orchestration of creation.

Chapter 13: The Flower of Life — Pattern of All Creation

"The Flower of Life is more than a symbol—it is a key. Within its elegant geometry lies the hidden architecture of all creation, waiting to be remembered."

Among all the figures in sacred geometry, few are as visually captivating or spiritually significant as the **Flower of Life**. This seemingly simple pattern of overlapping circles has been revered across cultures for millennia as a sacred map of creation, consciousness, and unity.

In this chapter, we explore the **structure**, **symbolism**, and **spiritual potency** of the Flower of Life, uncovering why it is often called the **geometric code of the universe**.

I. What Is the Flower of Life?

The Flower of Life is a geometrical figure composed of **evenly spaced, overlapping circles** arranged in a **hexagonal pattern**, where each circle's center lies on the circumference of six surrounding circles.

Key features:

- Typically formed from **19 full circles** enclosed in a larger circle
- Contains **multiple layers of symbolism**:
    - **Vesica Piscis**
    - **Seed of Life**
    - **Egg of Life**
    - **Fruit of Life**
    - **Metatron's Cube**

Each of these sub-patterns unlocks deeper insights into the **architecture of reality**.

II. The Structure of the Flower of Life

1. **The Vesica Piscis**: The first form—two overlapping circles—symbolizes **duality, union**, and **creation**.
2. **The Seed of Life**: Formed by seven interlocking circles, symbolizing the **seven days of creation**.
3. **The Flower of Life**: Expands the Seed into a **larger hexagonal pattern**—a cosmic blueprint.
4. **The Fruit of Life**: 13 inner circles from the Flower, acting as a **gateway** to **Metatron's Cube** and the **Platonic Solids**.
5. **Metatron's Cube**: A complex 3D pattern hidden within the Flower that reveals all **five Platonic Solids**, or the "building blocks of matter."

These nested forms symbolize the unfolding of creation—from **pure potential** to **manifested reality**.

III. Historical Presence Across Cultures

The Flower of Life has appeared throughout history and across civilizations:

- **Ancient Egypt**: Found inscribed on the walls of the Osirion temple in Abydos—one of the oldest and most mysterious appearances.
- **China** and **Tibet**: Used in sacred art and temple architecture.
- **India**: Incorporated into mandalas and yantras for spiritual activation.
- **Renaissance Europe**: Studied by **Leonardo da Vinci**, who explored its geometric and philosophical meanings.
- **Islamic Art**: Inspires complex tessellations and tile designs reflecting divine unity.
- **Kabbalah and the Tree of Life**: The Fruit of Life serves as a scaffold for the **Tree of Life**, linking Jewish mysticism with geometry.

Its appearance across **diverse traditions** is a testament to its **universal spiritual significance**.

IV. Symbolic and Spiritual Meaning

Symbol/Aspect	Interpretation
Circle	Unity, oneness, divine source
Overlap	Creation, relationship, interconnectedness
Flower pattern	Fertility, expansion, sacred beauty
Central symmetry	The still point in motion; divine balance
Hexagonal matrix	Order, cosmic structure, balance of opposites

The Flower of Life teaches us that **everything is connected**—all beings, ideas, and forms emerge from the same **divine origin**.

V. The Flower of Life and Sacred Geometry

Within the Flower of Life lie the **foundations of sacred geometry**:

- **Golden Ratio**: Found in the spacing between elements
- **Fibonacci Spiral**: Can be overlaid onto the expanding pattern
- **Platonic Solids**: Derived from Metatron's Cube, hidden within the Fruit of Life
- **Fractality**: A repeating pattern at all scales of creation
- **Toroidal Flow**: The circles reflect energy movement in vortex form

The Flower is more than a symbol—it's a **map of multidimensional reality**.

VI. Modern Interpretation and Use

1. Energy Healing & Meditation

- Used in energy work to **align chakras**, balance the **aura**, and enhance **spiritual connection**.
- Meditation on the Flower can deepen insight and activate higher states of awareness.

2. Art and Architecture

- Seen in visionary art, stained glass, and sacred architecture.
- Designers use its symmetry to invoke harmony and **cosmic resonance**.

3. Technology and Consciousness

- Some researchers believe the Flower encodes **unified field theory** or **quantum information**.
- It's used as a symbol of **new paradigm thinking**, integrating science and spirit.

VII. Drawing the Flower of Life

To connect with this sacred pattern, **drawing it by hand** is a powerful practice. Here's a simplified method:

1. **Start with a compass** and draw one circle.
2. Place the compass point on the circumference of that circle and draw a second circle.
3. Continue this process around the center point to create **six overlapping circles** (Seed of Life).
4. Expand outward in concentric rings until you reach the full **Flower of Life**.

Tip: As you draw, meditate on **unity, creation, and connection**—infuse your intention into the geometry.

VIII. Living the Flower of Life

To live in harmony with this pattern means:

- Recognizing the **interconnectedness** of all life
- Honoring both the **visible and invisible** realms
- Creating with **intention and balance**
- Aligning your personal growth with the **natural flow of the universe**

The Flower of Life is not only **a pattern to observe** but a **principle to embody**.

IX. Summary: The Geometry of Becoming

Element	Meaning
Seed of Life	Beginning of creation
Flower of Life	Expansion, pattern of all that exists
Fruit of Life	Gateway to structure and form
Metatron's Cube	Blueprint of physical and spiritual laws

Through this pattern, we remember that creation is not chaotic—it is a sacred unfolding of form, rhythm, and **divine intelligence**.

Chapter 14: The Seed, Egg, and Fruit of Life

"Just as a tree begins with a seed, so does the universe unfold from the simplest of geometric truths."

The Flower of Life is often celebrated for its beauty and mystery, but its power lies equally in its **sub-patterns**—the **Seed of Life**, **Egg of Life**, and **Fruit of Life**. These three nested stages reflect the **progressive unfolding of creation**, encoded in geometry.

This chapter dives deep into these forms, showing how they symbolize not only the structure of the universe but also the stages of personal and spiritual development.

I. The Seed of Life: Genesis and Potential

Structure and Composition

- Composed of **seven interlocking circles**, with one central circle and six surrounding it.
- Often referred to as the **"Genesis Pattern."**
- All circles share the same diameter and intersect at key points, forming a **flower-like design**.

Symbolism and Meaning

- Represents **the seven days of creation** in biblical tradition.
- A **symbol of potential**, like a seed before sprouting.
- Encodes the **Vesica Piscis** multiple times (symbol of duality and birth).
- Embodies the **first stage** in the geometric unfolding of reality.

Spiritual Interpretations

- Seven circles = seven chakras, seven musical notes, seven heavens.

- Meditating on the Seed of Life aligns one with the **source of creation**.
- Used in mystic traditions as a portal to **cosmic consciousness**.

In Nature and Science

- Reflected in cell division—**the first mitotic divisions** of a fertilized egg visually mirror the Seed of Life.
- Represents the balance of **structure and potential energy**.

II. The Egg of Life: The Blueprint of Life

Structure and Composition

- Formed when the Seed of Life expands into **eight spheres**: one central sphere and seven around it.
- In 3D space, it forms a **cube-like structure**, often called the **octahedral egg**.
- This is also known as the **first stage of embryonic development** in many living organisms.

Symbolism and Meaning

- Symbol of **fertilization, gestation, and early life**.
- Represents the **matrix of all biological life**.
- Encodes **harmonic ratios** found in music and vibration.
- Serves as the **structural basis** of the human body and DNA.

Scientific & Biological Correlations

- Seen in the **morphology of early embryonic cells** (blastomeres).
- The **Egg of Life** is a **3D structure** hidden within the 2D Flower of Life.
- Suggests that life itself follows a **geometric blueprint** from the very beginning.

Spiritual and Esoteric Uses

- In meditation, the Egg of Life is a tool for **awakening cellular memory**.

- Symbolizes the **sacred feminine**, fertility, and the divine capacity to create.

III. The Fruit of Life: The Matrix of Matter

Structure and Composition

- A complex pattern made of **13 circles** extracted from the center of the Flower of Life.
- The arrangement forms a **framework** upon which **Metatron's Cube** can be constructed.

Symbolism and Meaning

- Represents the **completion of creation** and the beginning of manifestation.
- The number 13 symbolizes:
    - **Unity and transformation**
    - The **13 original chakras** in some esoteric traditions
    - The **divine feminine** and lunar cycles (13 full moons per year)

Metatron's Cube and Platonic Solids

- When straight lines are drawn between the centers of each of the 13 circles, the result is **Metatron's Cube**.
- This contains all **five Platonic Solids**—the geometric forms that underlie all matter.
- Metatron's Cube is a **3D portal** into the understanding of physical and metaphysical laws.

Spiritual Applications

- Symbol of **divine knowledge and sacred order**.
- Often used in meditations for **protection, alignment, and activation**.
- Considered a **dimensional key** to access higher consciousness and the quantum nature of existence.

IV. From Seed to Fruit: The Cycle of Creation

Stage	Geometric Form	Symbolizes
Seed of Life	7 circles	Potential, genesis, the divine spark
Egg of Life	8 spheres (3D)	Gestation, early life, sacred memory
Fruit of Life	13 circles	Manifestation, order, cosmic design

These patterns represent more than steps in a sequence—they symbolize **a living process**. The seed becomes the egg, and the egg matures into the fruit. Just like in nature, geometry mirrors **growth, emergence, and fulfillment**.

V. Applying the Sacred Forms

1. Meditative Visualization

- Seed of Life: Visualize it in your heart center to connect to **divine potential**.
- Egg of Life: Use in deep meditations for **healing cellular trauma** and remembering your divine origin.
- Fruit of Life: Envision during manifestation practices or when calling in **divine structure** and wisdom.

2. Drawing Practice

- Draw each pattern step-by-step using a compass.
- Feel the energy shift as you move from one form to the next.
- Drawing them consciously is a sacred act of **co-creation with the universe**.

3. Life Reflection Exercise

Ask yourself:

- What seeds am I planting in my life?
- What am I gestating or nurturing quietly within?

- What fruits are ready to emerge, and how can I harvest them with grace?

VI. Summary: Geometry as the Sacred Spiral of Becoming

The Seed, Egg, and Fruit of Life are not only sacred geometric symbols; they are **mirrors of existence**. They teach us:

- That creation is not random—it is **ordered and intelligent**.
- That life emerges through **spirals, circles, and resonance**.
- That within every moment is the potential for **divine unfolding**.

By working with these patterns, we align ourselves with the **creative principle** of the universe. We become more than observers of sacred geometry—we become **participants in its unfolding story**.

Chapter 15: Metatron's Cube and the Blueprint of the Universe

"Geometry is the archetype of the beauty of the world."
— Johannes Kepler

At the heart of sacred geometry lies a mysterious and powerful figure known as **Metatron's Cube**—a shape that appears deceptively simple but encodes the most fundamental structures of matter, spirit, and cosmic intelligence. Born from the **Fruit of Life**, Metatron's Cube is said to contain the **blueprint of the universe**.

In this chapter, we will explore the **origin, construction, symbolism**, and **applications** of Metatron's Cube. We will also examine how it reveals the inner architecture of the cosmos—linking the **visible** and the **invisible**, the **material** and the **divine**.

I. Origin of Metatron's Cube

Metatron's Cube is a two-dimensional figure derived by connecting all **13 circles** of the **Fruit of Life** with straight lines. Though it appears flat, it encodes **three-dimensional structures** and embodies the geometry of **matter, energy**, and **consciousness**.

Construction:

1. Begin with the **Fruit of Life**—13 evenly spaced circles.
2. Draw straight lines from the center of each circle to the center of every other circle.
3. The resulting figure forms a complex pattern with **78 lines**.
4. Within this, the **five Platonic Solids** can be precisely found.

This process shows how **creation unfolds through connection**, structure, and proportion. It is not chaos—it is geometry.

II. The Archangel Metatron: Guardian of Sacred Geometry

Metatron's Cube is named after the **Archangel Metatron**, a figure found in Jewish mysticism (especially in Kabbalah) and other esoteric traditions.

Metatron's Roles:

- The **scribe of heaven**—recording all deeds in the Book of Life.
- The **bridge between divine and human**—the only angel said to have once been human (Enoch).
- Guardian of the **Tree of Life**, which is closely aligned with the structure of the cube.
- Overseer of **sacred geometry**, time, and spiritual laws.

In metaphysical teachings, Metatron's Cube is seen as a **divine instrument**, a geometrical expression of **universal consciousness**, and a portal to higher realms.

III. Geometry Within the Cube

One of the most astonishing aspects of Metatron's Cube is its ability to contain every one of the **five Platonic Solids**—the only five three-dimensional shapes in which all faces, edges, and angles are equal.

The Platonic Solids Embedded:

- **Tetrahedron** (Fire)
- **Hexahedron/Cube** (Earth)
- **Octahedron** (Air)
- **Dodecahedron** (Ether/Spirit)
- **Icosahedron** (Water)

Each of these is not just a physical structure, but a **symbol of elemental forces**, directions, seasons, and consciousness states.

Through Metatron's Cube, these solids can be:

- **Visualized**
- **Drawn**
- **Meditated upon**
- **Used as gateways** to understand the building blocks of matter and metaphysical energy

It serves as **proof** that the universe has a **mathematical architecture**—a sacred blueprint.

IV. Symbolism and Spiritual Meaning

Aspect of Metatron's Cube	Symbolic Meaning
13 circles	Unity, transformation, divine cycles
78 lines	Complexity from simplicity, complete connection
Hidden solids	The underlying structure of the material world

Aspect of Metatron's Cube	Symbolic Meaning
Central symmetry	Balance of polarities, spiritual center of creation
Outer hexagonal frame	Harmony, structure, the foundation of reality

In spiritual traditions, Metatron's Cube is used to:

- **Cleanse and protect** energy fields
- **Balance** masculine and feminine polarities
- Serve as a **map for ascension** and multidimensional awareness
- **Anchor divine light** into physical form

V. Practical Uses and Applications

1. Meditation and Visualization

- Place the image in your sacred space or altar.
- Focus on its symmetry to quiet the mind and activate **higher awareness**.
- Use it to connect with the **Archangel Metatron** or invoke **clarity and protection**.

2. Energy Healing

- Visualize the cube surrounding your body to cleanse and balance your aura.
- Practitioners often use it to **clear negative energies** and seal energetic leaks.

3. Manifestation

- Draw or meditate with Metatron's Cube to amplify your **intentions**.
- Its structure aligns your desire with the **natural order** of universal design.

4. Art and Architecture

- Used in **sacred design**, temple layouts, and mandalas.
- Inspires architects, artists, and philosophers seeking balance between form and spirit.

VI. Metatron's Cube and the Quantum Universe

Some modern thinkers and physicists see metaphysical parallels between Metatron's Cube and **quantum field theory, string theory,** and **sacred algorithms**:

- The cube may encode **vibrational fields, light geometry,** and **torus energy dynamics.**
- Its symmetry resonates with **non-locality**—the idea that all points are interconnected.
- The arrangement of energy and matter in the universe appears to follow a **holographic design**, which Metatron's Cube exemplifies.

Thus, Metatron's Cube serves as a **symbolic bridge** between **ancient mysticism** and **modern science.**

VII. Drawing Metatron's Cube: A Ritual of Creation

To draw it by hand:

1. Begin with the **13 circles** of the Fruit of Life.
2. Use a ruler to draw straight lines connecting the center of each circle to every other.
3. Highlight the **hidden Platonic Solids**.
4. Observe how complexity arises from **simple beginnings**.

This process becomes a **living meditation**—you aren't just drawing a shape, you are participating in the act of **cosmic creation.**

VIII. Summary: The Divine Blueprint

Metatron's Cube is more than a diagram—it is a **sacred architecture** through which the universe unfolds. It reminds us that:

- Matter is formed by **spirit moving through form**.
- Complexity arises from **divine simplicity**.
- All things are **connected through structure and vibration**.

To work with Metatron's Cube is to align with the **blueprint of life**—not as passive observers, but as conscious co-creators.

CONSTRUCTING METATRON'S CUBE

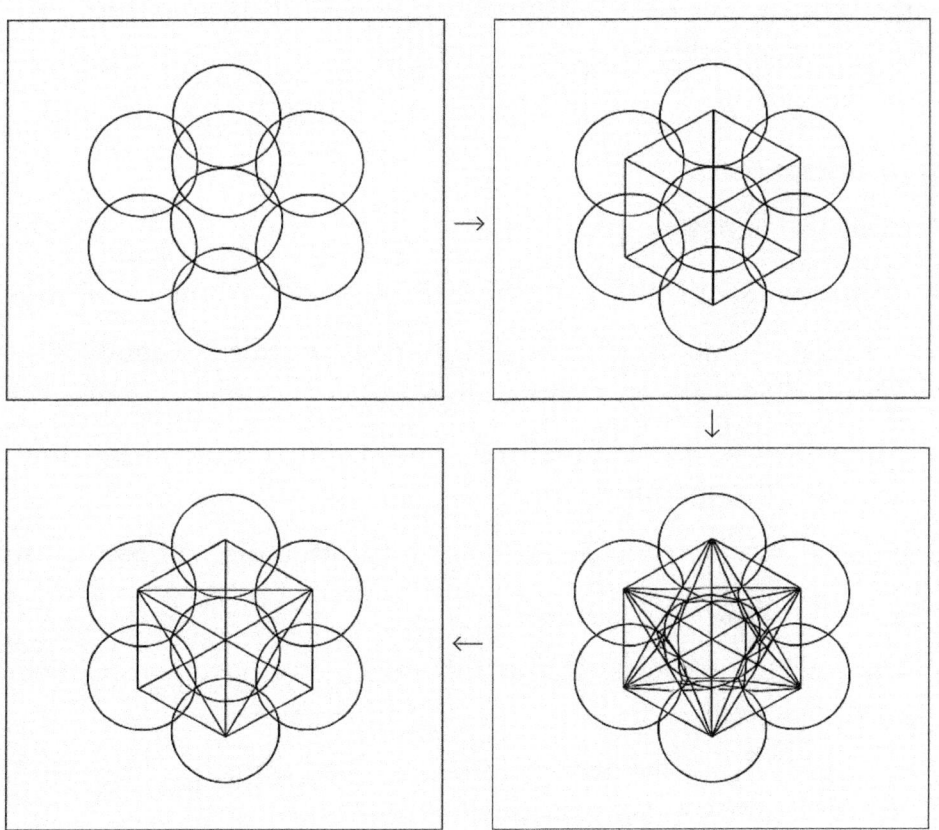

Chapter 16: The Sri Yantra and Eastern Sacred Geometry

"The yantra is a door to the absolute. It is the map of the cosmos and the human spirit, woven together through sacred proportion."
— Ancient Tantric Teaching

Sacred geometry is not confined to the West. Long before Metatron's Cube or the Platonic Solids were studied in Europe, the Eastern world developed its own sacred geometric systems—rich in symbolism, spirituality, and mathematical precision. Among the most profound of these is the **Sri Yantra**—a complex and revered symbol in Hindu and Tantric traditions.

The Sri Yantra is more than an object of meditation. It is considered the **embodiment of the cosmos**, a map to the divine, and a reflection of our inner universe. This chapter explores its construction, meaning, and transformative power, as well as other Eastern sacred geometric forms that have shaped spiritual practice for millennia.

I. What Is a Yantra?

Definition and Function

- **"Yantra"** (Sanskrit: यन्त्र) means "instrument," "machine," or "tool."
- In spiritual practice, a yantra is a **geometric diagram used for meditation, concentration, and ritual**.
- Functions like a **visual mantra**—a symbol that contains spiritual vibration and intention.
- Each yantra represents a specific **deity, principle, or cosmic force**.

Yantra vs. Mandala

- **Yantra**: More structured, mathematical, and focused on a specific deity or energy.
- **Mandala**: Typically more pictorial and used across Buddhist and Hindu traditions as a broader symbol of wholeness.

II. The Sri Yantra: Geometry of the Goddess

Structure and Components

The **Sri Yantra** (also called the Shri Chakra) is a sacred symbol composed of **nine interlocking triangles** radiating from a central point (bindu):

- **4 upward-pointing triangles**: Represent Shiva (masculine energy)
- **5 downward-pointing triangles**: Represent Shakti (feminine energy)

These nine triangles form a total of **43 smaller triangles**, creating a web of interconnection symbolizing the **entire cosmos**.

Other key elements:

- **Bindu (dot)**: The central point; pure consciousness or source.
- **Lotus petals**: Often surrounding the triangles, representing divine unfolding.
- **Outer square (bhupura)**: Enclosure symbolizing the material world with gates at the four cardinal directions.

Symbolic Interpretation

- **Union of Shiva and Shakti**: Divine masculine and feminine forces merging into one.
- **Cosmic manifestation**: The movement from undifferentiated unity (bindu) to multiplicity and form (outer square).
- **Spiritual journey**: From the material world through layers of complexity back to divine simplicity and union.

III. The Sri Yantra as a Spiritual Technology

The Sri Yantra is used not just as a symbol, but as an active **spiritual technology**—a sacred map that mirrors both the **macrocosm (the universe)** and **microcosm (the self)**.

Uses and Benefits

- **Meditation aid**: Calms the mind, enhances focus, and harmonizes energies.

- **Energetic amplifier**: Believed to attract prosperity, healing, and spiritual awakening.
- **Ritual tool**: Used in tantric puja (worship), initiations, and ceremonies.

The Path of Return

The nine levels or **avaranas** (enclosures) of the Sri Yantra represent stages of spiritual awakening. The practitioner's journey is a **movement inward**—through the layers of illusion and complexity—toward unity at the bindu.

IV. Mathematical Precision and Cosmic Order

The Sri Yantra is one of the most **mathematically sophisticated** symbols in sacred geometry. Its construction has challenged mathematicians for centuries due to the precise placement and interlocking of triangles.

Mathematical Marvels:

- Requires **precise angles** and **symmetry** to form a perfect diagram.
- The most accurate constructions create triangles in the **golden ratio**—just like Western sacred forms.
- The layout aligns with **harmonic proportions**, **fractal scaling**, and **vortex dynamics**.

Cosmic Resonance:

- Symbolizes the **geometry of vibration** and the structure of energy in space.
- Considered a **blueprint of reality** in Indian metaphysics—much like Metatron's Cube in the West.

V. Drawing the Sri Yantra: A Spiritual Discipline

Creating the Sri Yantra is a meditative act that demands **concentration, precision, and patience**.

Traditional Drawing Sequence:

1. Start with the **bindu**—the divine source point.

2. Construct the **interlocking triangles** with careful spacing.
3. Add the **lotus petals**—8 inner and 16 outer.
4. Finish with the **bhupura**—the enclosing square with gates.
5. Color or gild with sacred pigments (often red, gold, and blue).

In some traditions, the drawing is done as a **ceremonial practice** lasting several days or weeks. The final diagram is treated as a **living embodiment** of the divine.

VI. Other Eastern Sacred Geometries

1. Mandala (Tibetan and Hindu)

- Symmetrical, circular designs used for meditation and ritual.
- Represent the **universe**, the **self**, and the **divine abode**.
- Often used in Tibetan Buddhism to teach **impermanence**, as they are ritually created and destroyed.

2. Vastu Purusha Mandala (Vedic Architecture)

- Grid-based geometric system used in **Vastu Shastra**, the Indian science of architecture.
- Aligns homes and temples with **cosmic energies**, similar to Feng Shui.

3. Chakra Geometry

- Each **chakra** is symbolized by a geometric form (lotus petals, triangles, circles).
- Geometric representations help visualize and **activate energy centers** in the body.

VII. Bridging East and West

Though developed independently, Eastern and Western sacred geometries reveal **universal truths**:

Concept	Eastern Geometry (Sri Yantra)	Western Geometry (Metatron's Cube)
Central symbol	Bindu (point of origin)	Central circle/intersection
Sacred number	9 triangles / 43 sub-triangles	13 circles / 78 lines
Dimensionality	Flat diagram encoding multidimensionality	2D figure revealing 3D solids
Divine union	Shiva & Shakti	Masculine & feminine principles
Goal	Self-realization / divine union	Cosmic order / spiritual awakening

This alignment shows that **sacred geometry is a universal language**—one that transcends culture and dogma to reveal the essence of all creation.

VIII. Summary: The Diagram of Divine Design

The Sri Yantra is not just a diagram—it is a **living portal** into the infinite. It shows that the universe is not chaotic, but **harmoniously ordered**. Through triangles, circles, and nested layers, it mirrors the **dance of creation**, the **journey of the soul**, and the **union of duality into oneness**.

To meditate on the Sri Yantra is to come face to face with your **divine origin**—to step into a field of sacred energy that transcends time, form, and mind.

1. Draw the dot

2. Add the triagans

3. Encolose in lotuses

4. Draw the outer square

Chapter 17: Labyrinths and Mandalas — Paths to the Center

"Your sacred space is where you can find yourself again and again."
— Joseph Campbell

All sacred geometry invites us to recognize patterns of order, beauty, and unity within the complexity of the world. Yet few geometric forms are as deeply meditative and symbolically rich as **labyrinths** and **mandalas**. These are more than designs—they are tools for journeying inward, connecting the seeker with the center of being, both within the self and the universe.

In this chapter, we explore labyrinths and mandalas as ancient, cross-cultural forms of sacred geometry. While they differ in form and function, both serve as **maps for spiritual pilgrimage**, offering the practitioner a symbolic path to transformation, healing, and union with the divine.

I. Understanding the Labyrinth: A Journey inwards

What Is a Labyrinth?

Unlike a maze, which confuses and misleads, a **labyrinth has only one path**—a single, non-branching route that winds to the center and back out again. It is not a puzzle to be solved but a **path to be walked**.

Labyrinths date back thousands of years and have been found in:

- Ancient Crete (e.g., the myth of the Minotaur)
- Native American petroglyphs
- Medieval European cathedrals
- Celtic and Norse stone carvings
- Hindu yantras (some traced with the feet in rituals)

Symbolism of the Labyrinth

- **The Path**: Life's spiritual journey with its twists and turns.
- **The Center**: Divine presence, truth, or enlightenment.
- **The Return**: Rebirth, transformation, and integration of insight.

Walking the labyrinth mirrors the process of spiritual initiation:

1. **Release** – Letting go of distractions and ego on the inward journey.
2. **Receive** – Meeting the stillness and wisdom at the center.
3. **Return** – Bringing that insight back to the world.

Sacred Geometry in Labyrinths

Most labyrinths are based on circular, spiral, or grid-based geometries. Famous examples include:

- **The Chartres Cathedral Labyrinth** (France): An 11-circuit pattern built into the floor, reflecting the celestial and terrestrial alignment of Gothic architecture.
- **Classical Seven-Circuit Labyrinth**: Based on a seed pattern that can be drawn using simple geometric constructions.
- **Contemporary Labyrinths**: Often modeled using Fibonacci spirals, vesica piscis ratios, or fractal curves.

II. The Mandala: Sacred Circle of Wholeness

What Is a Mandala?

A **mandala** (Sanskrit: "circle") is a geometric configuration of symbols, often arranged in concentric patterns, used in Hinduism, Buddhism, and other spiritual traditions as a **map of the cosmos**, **the mind**, and **the divine**.

Unlike labyrinths, which are walked, mandalas are typically **visualized, drawn, or meditated upon**. However, both represent a movement toward **centeredness and integration**.

Core Features of Mandalas

- **Central Point (Bindu)**: The origin, unity, or Godhead.
- **Radial Symmetry**: Reflecting balance, harmony, and completeness.
- **Nested Circles and Squares**: Representing layers of existence or realms of consciousness.
- **Gates at the Cardinal Directions**: Pathways into the sacred space.

Mandalas can be:

- Personal (inner psychology, chakra diagrams)
- Cosmic (symbolizing the universe)
- Ritual (used in ceremonies or initiations)

Mandalas Across Cultures

- **Tibetan Mandalas**: Created with colored sand to represent deities, realms, or mantras—then ritually destroyed to symbolize impermanence.
- **Hindu Yantras**: Abstract geometric mandalas, such as the **Sri Yantra**, representing specific deities and energies.
- **Christian Rose Windows**: Circular stained glass windows in cathedrals, often with twelve-fold or symmetrical designs symbolizing divine order.
- **Native American Medicine Wheels**: Circular symbols mapping directions, elements, and spiritual teachings.

III. The Shared Essence: Path, Center, Unity

Despite differences in culture and practice, labyrinths and mandalas share profound commonalities:

Element	Labyrinth	Mandala
Shape	Circular or spiral	Circular, radial symmetry
Movement	Walking inward and outward	Gaze or focus inward
Symbolism	Life journey, initiation, transformation	Cosmic order, unity, wholeness
Center	Destination of journey	Source of all creation
Use	Meditation through movement	Meditation through sight and visualization

Element	Labyrinth	Mandala
Purpose	Healing, integration, spiritual insight	Realization, contemplation, divine presence

Both serve as **sacred containers**—spaces in which the spiritual journey can unfold. They allow the practitioner to move from the outer world to the inner sanctuary, from multiplicity to unity.

IV. Creating and Using These Sacred Forms

Drawing a Mandala

1. Begin with a circle.
2. Divide it radially (often into 4, 8, or 12 segments).
3. Add concentric circles, geometric motifs (triangles, lotus petals, grids).
4. Work from the center outward or inward as your intuition guides.
5. Infuse each stage with **intention and focus**.

Drawing a mandala is a powerful act of **mindful creativity** and **visual prayer**.

Walking or Tracing a Labyrinth

1. Find or draw a simple 7- or 11-circuit labyrinth (these can be made with rope, stones, or chalk).
2. Before entering, set an intention or ask a question.
3. Walk slowly, breathing deeply, letting thoughts arise and fall.
4. Pause at the center. Be still.
5. Return with awareness of any insights or emotional shifts.

Even tracing a labyrinth with your finger or eyes can have a calming and clarifying effect.

V. Inner Pilgrimage: Why These Symbols Matter Today

In today's fast-paced, fractured world, labyrinths and mandalas offer something rare: a **pathway home**. They reconnect us to:

- Our **inner stillness**
- A sense of **sacred space**
- The rhythm and order of **natural life**

These are not just historical or cultural curiosities. They are **living templates** that help us process grief, release anxiety, heal trauma, and remember who we are.

To walk a labyrinth or gaze upon a mandala is to be reminded that **the divine is not distant**—it is found in the **very center of our being**. In the language of sacred geometry, the circle, the spiral, and the radial star all point toward the **One** within the many.

Whether you walk the path or draw it with reverence, these sacred forms will meet you where you are and guide you to where you belong: the center.

Part III: Sacred Geometry in the Natural and Human World

Chapter 18: Geometry in Nature — The Hidden Order of Life

"Geometry will draw the soul toward truth."
— Plato

Nature may appear wild and chaotic at first glance, but beneath the surface lies a deep, intelligent structure. This structure is **geometric**—subtle, elegant, and universal. The spiral of a galaxy, the branching of a tree, the shape of a snowflake—all reveal a silent order, a sacred architecture of life itself.

In this chapter, we'll explore how **geometry governs the living world**, from cellular patterns to weather systems. By understanding these patterns, we deepen our connection with nature—and with the creative intelligence behind it all.

I. The Geometry of Growth and Form

All life unfolds according to laws of proportion, balance, and pattern. This isn't coincidence—it's **mathematics in motion**.

1. The Fibonacci Sequence in Nature

- A mathematical pattern where each number is the sum of the two preceding ones:
  0, 1, 1, 2, 3, 5, 8, 13, 21…
- Found in:
  - Petal arrangements on flowers (e.g., lilies = 3, buttercups = 5, daisies = 21+)
  - Pinecones, pineapples, and sunflower seed spirals
  - Rabbit population modeling
  - DNA helices and phyllotaxis (leaf arrangement)

2. The Golden Ratio ($\Phi \approx 1.618$)

- Closely linked with the Fibonacci sequence.

- Found in:
    - The proportions of leaves and stems
    - Nautilus shells
    - The human face and body
    - The branching of trees and veins in leaves

These proportions help organisms **grow efficiently, conserve energy, and optimize exposure** to sunlight, water, and nutrients.

II. Spirals, Fractals, and the Pattern of Expansion

1. Logarithmic Spirals

- Found in snail shells, hurricanes, galaxies, and ram's horns.
- Unlike circles, they grow **outward while retaining the same shape**, reflecting expansion without distortion.
- Embody **growth, evolution, and movement**—a universal pattern of life.

2. Fractals in Nature

- Fractals are **self-similar patterns**—structures that repeat on increasingly smaller or larger scales.
- Examples:
    - Tree branches
    - River networks
    - Blood vessels and lungs
    - Snowflakes and lightning bolts
- Fractals reflect how **simple rules create complex systems**, and they allow organisms to maximize space and efficiency with minimal energy.

III. Sacred Geometry at the Cellular and Atomic Levels

Even the smallest units of life are designed with sacred patterns.

1. DNA: The Twisted Ladder

- DNA's double helix structure encodes **geometric ratios**, including the **Golden Ratio** between spiral turns and width.
- The 5-carbon sugar ring in DNA forms a **pentagonal** molecule—resonating with the pentagon's sacred proportions.

2. Cell Division and the Vesica Piscis

- The first division of a fertilized egg forms a shape called the **Vesica Piscis**—two overlapping circles, symbolizing union and creation.
- Further divisions follow the **Platonic solids** pattern of organization, especially the **tetrahedron** and **cube**.

IV. The Geometry of Animals and Plants

1. Symmetry in Animals

- Radial symmetry (e.g., starfish, jellyfish): Echoes the circle, associated with the center and unity.
- Bilateral symmetry (e.g., mammals, humans): Reflects balance and duality.

2. Geometric Design in Insects

- Honeybees build **hexagonal honeycombs**—the most efficient shape for storing maximum honey with minimal wax.
- Spiders weave webs in radial, concentric patterns—often with **fractal precision**.

3. Plants and Sacred Proportion

- Most leaves grow in spiral arrangements around stems, known as **phyllotaxis**, optimizing light absorption.
- Many flowers express **mandala-like symmetry**, with petals arranged in multiples of Fibonacci numbers.

V. Geometry of the Earth and Elements

1. Crystals and Minerals

- Crystals form in **precise geometric structures**, such as cubes (salt), hexagons (quartz), and octahedrons (fluorite).
- Reflect sacred solids and lattice symmetry embedded in nature.

2. Water and Snowflakes

- Water molecules form a **hexagonal crystal** lattice when frozen.
- No two snowflakes are alike, yet all express **sixfold radial symmetry**—a sacred signature of balance.

3. Weather Patterns

- Hurricanes and cyclones form spirals.
- Tornadoes, wave patterns, and even planetary storms (e.g., Jupiter's Great Red Spot) reflect **rotational symmetry**.

VI. Sacred Geometry in Human Anatomy

- The **human body** follows the Golden Ratio in numerous proportions:
    - Height to navel / navel to crown
    - Finger bone ratios
    - Facial structure
- The **five-pointed star** (pentagram) appears naturally in the proportions of the human body—Leonardo da Vinci's *Vitruvian Man* is based on these ideals.

VII. Seeing Nature as the Divine Architect

When we observe nature with sacred geometry in mind, we begin to see the world differently:

- Patterns repeat with precision and intention.
- Chaos gives way to hidden harmony.

- The universe becomes a **living mandala**, always in motion yet rooted in order.

This perception transforms how we relate to our environment. We begin to **see the divine in the ordinary**, and realize that geometry is not just in textbooks—it's in **leaves, clouds, mountains, and stars**.

VIII. Summary: Living in Alignment with the Pattern

Nature teaches us that beauty, balance, and structure are not separate from life—they are the **essence of life**. Sacred geometry reveals that everything is connected through proportion, rhythm, and form.

By attuning ourselves to these patterns:

- We gain insight into **the intelligence of creation**.
- We deepen our connection to **the Earth and cosmos**.
- We remember that we are not separate from nature, but **expressions of the same divine geometry**.

Chapter 19: The Human Body — The Divine Proportion Within

"Man is the measure of all things."
— Protagoras

The human body is more than flesh, bones, and sinew. It is a **masterwork of proportion**, a living testament to sacred geometry in action. Every limb, organ, and facial feature speaks the language of form and function with astonishing precision. Far from random, the design of the human body echoes cosmic principles—reflections of the divine blueprint manifest in physical form.

In this chapter, we will explore the sacred geometries embedded in the body: the **Golden Ratio**, the **Fibonacci sequence**, the **five-pointed star**, **chakra alignment**, and more. As we unveil these inner harmonies, we come to understand ourselves not only as biological beings, but as sacred architecture in motion.

I. The Golden Ratio and the Human Form

The Golden Ratio (Φ ≈ 1.618) is often called the "divine proportion" for its widespread presence in art, architecture, and nature. The human body, too, expresses this mysterious constant.

Proportional Examples in the Human Body:

- **Height to navel : Navel to crown** = ~1.618
- **Forearm to hand** = ~1.618
- **Length of each finger segment** follows the Fibonacci sequence
- **Facial proportions**:
    - Distance between the eyes vs. width of the head
    - Width of lips vs. width of nose
    - Placement of eyes, nose, and mouth align closely to Phi divisions

These ratios are not merely aesthetic—they often represent **optimal structural balance**, aiding movement, breathing, and sensory perception.

II. The Vitruvian Man: Geometry of the Whole

Leonardo da Vinci's famous drawing, the *Vitruvian Man*, is more than artistic genius—it is a geometric revelation.

Key Concepts Behind the Drawing:

- Based on the work of **Vitruvius**, a Roman architect who believed a well-proportioned human body mirrored the ideal architectural form.
- The drawing places a man within both a **circle** (symbolizing heaven/spirit) and a **square** (symbolizing earth/matter).
- The span of the arms equals the body's height; the center of the circle is the **navel**, suggesting the human being as the **microcosm** of the universe.

This encapsulates the **Hermetic principle**: *"As above, so below".* The body becomes a divine compass, harmonizing heaven and earth.

III. The Five-Pointed Star (Pentagram) in the Body

The pentagram is one of the most sacred symbols in geometry—and the human body reflects its proportions.

Symbolic Associations:

- **Head, two arms**, and **two legs** form a five-pointed star when the body is outstretched.
- The **angles** of a pentagram contain the **Golden Ratio** throughout.
- Ancient cultures, including the Pythagoreans, saw the pentagram as a symbol of **life, health**, and **cosmic order**.

By embodying this star, we literally wear the signature of sacred proportion.

IV. Chakras: Vertical Geometry of Energy

The **chakra system**, originating in Indian spiritual traditions, describes **seven energy centers** aligned along the spine, from the base to the crown.

Geometric Significance:

Each chakra is associated with:

- A **specific geometric shape** (e.g., triangle, lotus petal count)
- A **frequency, color**, and **element**
- **Mandalas**, often used in visualization and meditation, mirror the geometric unfolding of these centers.

The alignment of chakras follows the **vertical axis** of the human body, reflecting the **central axis mundi** or world tree—a spiritual spine connecting heaven and earth.

V. Sacred Geometry in Anatomy and Movement

Geometry isn't limited to proportions—it governs how the body **moves**, **balances**, and **functions**.

Skeletal Symmetry:

- Bilateral symmetry governs our **left/right balance**, promoting harmony and coordination.
- The **spine** is an S-curve—a form of natural engineering that supports upright posture and shock absorption.

Dynamic Movement:

- **Walking and running** generate spirals through the rotation of hips and shoulders.
- The body moves through **arcs, rotations, and waves**, reflecting **spiral dynamics** found in DNA, galaxies, and seashells.

VI. DNA: The Molecular Spiral

The **double helix** structure of DNA is a literal spiral staircase of life. It reflects:

- **Phi-based proportions** between the helix turns and diameter
- A **five-carbon sugar backbone**, aligning it with the **pentagon**
- The unfolding of genetic information through repeating, harmonic sequences—sacred geometry at the microscopic scale

---

VII. Embodied Geometry in Art, Dance, and Ritual

Human beings have long mirrored sacred geometry through **body-based practices**:

- **Yoga postures** (asanas) replicate geometric forms to align the body and subtle energies.
- **Classical dance** forms (e.g., Bharatanatyam, ballet) use geometric spacing, symmetry, and directional movements.
- **Martial arts**, such as Tai Chi and Kung Fu, are based on **circular and spiral movements**, optimizing flow and harmony.

- **Mudras** (hand gestures) form mini-geometric circuits in the body to channel energy.

These practices aren't symbolic—they're **embodied blueprints**, activating sacred design through physical form.

VIII. The Body as Temple

Many spiritual traditions regard the human body as a **temple of the divine**:

- In **Christianity**, the body is "a temple of the Holy Spirit."
- In **Yoga**, the body is a vehicle for enlightenment and union with Brahman.
- In **alchemy**, the human form contains both the elements and the philosopher's stone—symbolizing spiritual transformation.

Seeing the body through the lens of sacred geometry **restores reverence** for our physical being, not as flawed or fallen, but as **holy, mathematical, and magnificent**.

IX. Summary: The Divine Within

To understand sacred geometry in the human body is to see ourselves as part of a larger pattern—one that reflects the **structure of the universe itself**. Every breath, every gesture, every cell expresses the **Divine Pattern**.

By recognizing and honoring this geometry:

- We align more fully with the flow of life.
- We reclaim the body as a sacred vessel.
- We begin to live from a place of **centeredness, symmetry, and soul**.

Chapter 20: Sacred Architecture — Temples, Cathedrals, and Pyramids

---

"Architecture is frozen music."
— Johann Wolfgang von Goethe

Across cultures and continents, ancient builders erected structures that not only withstood time but echoed the rhythms of the cosmos. From the Great Pyramid of Giza to the soaring vaults of Gothic cathedrals and the mandala-like precision of Eastern temples, these buildings are more than places of worship — they are **geometric resonators, energy amplifiers**, and **gateways to the divine**.

Sacred architecture uses **geometry**, **proportion**, and **orientation** not just for beauty or structure, but to invoke **spiritual presence**. In this chapter, we explore how humanity has harnessed geometry to build temples of stone that mirror the temples of spirit.

I. The Foundations of Sacred Architecture

Sacred architecture is distinct from secular construction in key ways:

Core Characteristics:

- Built on **sacred ratios** (e.g. Golden Ratio, Pi, square root of 2)
- Oriented to **celestial alignments** (solstices, equinoxes, star risings)
- Use of **symbolic forms** (circles, squares, octagons, pyramids)
- Designed to **evoke transcendence** through space, light, and proportion

These structures serve as **harmonic environments** where mind, body, and spirit align with the cosmos.

II. The Pyramids of Egypt: Earth Meets Sky

The Great Pyramid of Giza is a mathematical marvel and one of the earliest known examples of sacred geometry applied at monumental scale.

Geometric Principles:

- Height to base ratio approximates **Pi (π)**:
  $2\pi \times$ radius = circumference → Height = radius

- The slope of the pyramid encodes the **Golden Ratio (Φ)**.
- Aligns precisely with **cardinal directions** (north, south, east, west).
- Incorporates **stellar alignment**: shafts point to Orion and Sirius.

Symbolic Interpretation:

- The square base represents **earth**, the pointed top **spirit**—a pyramid is thus a **spiritual ascension** tool.
- Designed as a **cosmic resurrection machine** for the pharaoh's soul.

III. Greek and Roman Temples: Harmonic Proportion

The classical temples of Greece and Rome, such as the **Parthenon**, embody **mathematical purity**.

Architectural Features:

- Use of the **Golden Rectangle** in facade and floor plans.
- **Doric, Ionic**, and **Corinthian columns** follow fixed proportional rules (modules).
- **Symmetry and balance** are core to conveying divine order.

Sacred Symbolism:

- Temples were constructed as **embodiments of gods**, with inner sanctums (naos) reserved for the divine presence.
- The layout often mirrored the **human body**, reflecting the microcosm-macrocosm principle.

IV. Gothic Cathedrals: Stone as Light

The Gothic cathedral is among the most powerful examples of sacred geometry in the Western world.

Key Geometric Elements:

- **Pointed arches** and **ribbed vaults** mirror **triangular geometry** (symbolic of the Trinity).

- Floor plans often based on the **cross** or the **vesica piscis**.
- Use of **sacred numbers**: e.g., 3 (Trinity), 4 (elements), 7 (sacraments), 12 (apostles).

Famous Examples:

- **Chartres Cathedral**: Its rose windows display **mandala-like symmetry**, and the labyrinth in its nave reflects a **spiritual journey to the center**.
- **Notre-Dame de Paris**: Its construction echoes **celestial harmonics**, with proportions inspired by **music theory**.

Spiritual Function:

- Light streaming through **stained glass** was not just decorative, but an **alchemical medium**—transmuting stone into spirit.
- The buildings themselves were **cosmic diagrams**, facilitating transcendence through space.

V. Eastern Temples: Mandalas in Stone

In India, Tibet, China, and Southeast Asia, temples are often constructed as **three-dimensional mandalas**, expressions of the universe in physical form.

Hindu Temples:

- Based on the **Vastu Purusha Mandala**, a geometric grid aligning the structure with cardinal directions and cosmic forces.
- Central sanctum (garbhagriha) represents the **seed point of creation** (bindu).
- Tower (shikhara) mirrors **Mount Meru**, the mythic axis mundi.

Buddhist Stupas and Pagodas:

- Symbolize the **Buddha's body, speech, and mind** through form.
- The **dome shape** embodies the womb of the cosmos; the **spire** points upward to enlightenment.

- Structures like **Borobudur** in Java are **pilgrimage mandalas**, walked in concentric levels representing spiritual ascent.

Chinese and Japanese Temples:

- Emphasize **yin-yang balance**, the **Five Elements**, and **Feng Shui**.
- Layouts align with **earth's energy lines** (dragon veins), integrating **heaven, earth, and humanity**.

VI. Islamic Geometry: Unity through Pattern

Islamic sacred architecture avoids figurative imagery and instead embraces **pure geometry** as a path to the infinite.

Design Elements:

- **Tessellations, arabesques,** and **calligraphy** use complex geometry to represent **infinite unity (Tawhid)**.
- **Domes and arches** are constructed with precise mathematical formulas.
- Use of **symmetry and repetition** reflects the eternal nature of the divine.

Examples:

- **The Alhambra (Spain)**: Walls are covered in **geometric mosaics**, many based on **eight-fold** and **twelve-fold** symmetry.
- **The Dome of the Rock (Jerusalem)**: Built on a **central plan**, its octagonal geometry symbolizes regeneration and the cosmic order.

VII. Mesoamerican and Native Traditions

Sacred geometry is also present in the **temples and ceremonial sites** of the Americas.

Mayan and Aztec Pyramids:

- Stepped pyramids (e.g., Chichen Itza) align with **solar cycles** and **equinoxes**.

- Geometry encoded timekeeping: structures served as **calendrical observatories**.

Native North American Sites:

- **Medicine wheels, stone circles**, and **earthworks** reflect **solar and lunar alignments**.
- Built with awareness of **geometric harmony** and **spiritual power** of landforms.

VIII. Proportion, Resonance, and Energy

Beyond visual harmony, sacred structures are built to **resonate**.

Acoustic Geometry:

- Spaces like cathedrals and temples often exhibit **perfect acoustics**, amplifying chants and prayers.
- Architecture becomes **sonic geometry** — geometry that sings.

Energetic Alignment:

- Many temples are built on **geomagnetic hotspots**, **ley lines**, or **crosspoints of telluric currents**.
- The goal: to **bridge heaven and earth**, using the building as a tuning fork for spiritual energy.

IX. Summary: Living Temples, Living Geometry

Sacred architecture is not about bricks and mortar—it's about **meaning, measure, and memory**. These structures are maps of the universe, symbols of the soul, and tools for transformation.

They teach us:

- That **space can be sacred** when formed with intention.
- That **geometry is a spiritual language**, not just a mathematical one.
- That we too can become **temples of harmony**, built from the same divine proportions.

Chapter 21: Geometry in Art, Music, and Sound

"Where there is matter, there is geometry."
— Johannes Kepler

Art, music, and sound are more than creative expressions — they are visual and auditory reflections of the universe's hidden structure. Throughout history, humanity has used the **language of geometry** to create beauty that harmonizes the senses and lifts the soul. Whether in the spiral of a painter's brush, the rhythm of a drumbeat, or the harmonics of a string, **form and frequency dance in unison.**

In this chapter, we explore how sacred geometry manifests in **visual art**, **music theory**, and **vibrational science**, revealing that what we see and hear is deeply interconnected through the universal language of proportion, resonance, and pattern.

I. Visual Art and the Golden Frame

From classical to contemporary, sacred geometry has guided artists in creating visual masterpieces that communicate spiritual truths.

A. The Golden Ratio in Art

- **Leonardo da Vinci** used Phi (Φ) extensively — in *The Last Supper*, *Vitruvian Man*, and *Mona Lisa*, faces and compositions are proportioned according to the Golden Rectangle.
- **Michelangelo**, **Raphael**, and **Botticelli** all embedded sacred ratios in their Renaissance works.
- **Modern artists** like Salvador Dalí and Mondrian also employed geometric balance in layout and structure.

The Golden Ratio creates **visual harmony** that feels natural and pleasing to the eye, echoing the innate patterns of nature.

B. Sacred Mandalas and Symmetry

- Mandalas — found in Hindu, Buddhist, and Indigenous cultures — are **geometric diagrams of the cosmos**, often based on radial symmetry.
- Used in meditation and ritual, mandalas reflect the **fractal nature** of existence: self-replicating patterns from micro to macro.
- **Islamic geometric art** emphasizes tessellation and repetition to express infinite divine unity without representational imagery.

C. Geometry in Architecture as Art

- Structures like the **Rose Window** in Gothic cathedrals are both architectural and artistic — perfect expressions of radial geometry and light.
- Ancient mosaics, stained glass, and mosaics often used **six-fold symmetry**, **spirals**, and **fractal branching**.

II. Music and the Mathematics of Harmony

Music is structured vibration. Behind melody and rhythm lies an invisible lattice of ratios, intervals, and harmonics — all of which are inherently geometric.

A. Pythagoras and the Music of the Spheres

- Pythagoras discovered that musical intervals correspond to **simple whole-number ratios**:
    - Octave: 2:1
    - Fifth: 3:2
    - Fourth: 4:3
- He taught that celestial bodies emit their own vibrations — the **"music of the spheres"** — inaudible to the human ear but mathematically precise.

B. Harmonics and Geometry

- A vibrating string produces **harmonic overtones**, each related by exact ratios.

- These harmonics create **standing wave patterns**, which can be visualized geometrically as nodes and antinodes.
- **Wave interference patterns** — visualized in Chladni plates (see next section) — display symmetrical forms, linking sound directly to shape.

C. Musical Scales and Sacred Numbers

- The **diatonic scale** is built on ratios derived from sacred numbers: 3, 4, 5, 6, 8.
- In Indian classical music, **ragas** often relate to specific times of day and are said to correspond to planetary energies — musical astrology.

III. Cymatics: Seeing Sound

Cymatics is the study of **visible sound** — patterns created by frequencies as they move through matter.

A. What Is Cymatics?

- When sand, water, or particles are vibrated by sound on a surface, they organize into **geometric patterns**.
- **Ernst Chladni** was one of the first to experiment with sound and sand on metal plates in the 18th century.
- **Hans Jenny**, a 20th-century Swiss doctor, coined the term "cymatics" and documented hundreds of patterns, revealing a clear relationship between **frequency and form**.

B. Observations

- **Low frequencies** produce simple shapes (circles, triangles).
- **Higher frequencies** generate increasingly complex mandalas and fractal-like patterns.
- These forms are **not random**; they are shaped by the **laws of vibration** and **resonant frequency**.

C. Implications for Sacred Geometry

- Sound is a **creative force** — it organizes matter into order.
- In many traditions, **creation myths** begin with sound (e.g., "In the beginning was the Word").
- Cymatics offers a modern, scientific lens on ancient truths — that **sound is formative**.

IV. Sound Healing and Vibrational Geometry

Beyond theory, sound and geometry are being used today for **healing and transformation**.

A. Sound Therapy and Resonance

- Instruments like **singing bowls, gongs, didgeridoos**, and **tuning forks** create frequencies that influence brain waves and cellular structures.
- Each chakra is believed to vibrate at a specific frequency; sound can **restore coherence** to these energetic centers.

B. Binaural Beats and Harmonic Tuning

- Listening to slightly different tones in each ear creates a **binaural beat**, entraining brain activity into **alpha, theta, or delta states**.
- Ancient instruments were often **tuned to 432 Hz**, said to resonate more harmoniously with the natural world than the standard 440 Hz.

C. Visualizing Healing Sound

- Through cymatics, sound can be "tuned" to create **intentional forms** for healing, balance, and spiritual activation.
- **Sacred chant** and **mantra** practices rely on these same principles, using the voice to shape space.

V. Unifying Art, Sound, and Geometry

Throughout history, the **great geniuses** — Pythagoras, Leonardo, Kepler, and more — saw no division between art, music, and math. All were expressions of **universal harmony**.

Examples of Interwoven Disciplines:

- **Da Vinci** explored the geometry of proportion in both anatomical drawings and musical theories.
- **Kepler's planetary model** was based on **musical intervals** between planetary orbits — a true **harmony of the spheres**.
- In traditional mandala creation, **sound and mantra** accompany the **precise laying of geometric forms** — showing their inseparability.

Art and sound aren't distractions from the spiritual path — they are sacred tools for understanding and experiencing **the Divine Pattern**.

VI. Summary: The Senses as Portals to Sacred Form

When we see art or hear music that moves us, we're often responding to something **unseen** — the presence of sacred geometry encoded within.

- Art **visualizes** harmony.
- Music **audibilizes** geometry.
- Sound and form together **activate** higher consciousness.

As we train our senses to recognize these deeper patterns, we awaken to a world of beauty, symmetry, and interconnection. Every painting, every melody, every vibration becomes a **portal to the sacred**.

Chapter 22: Cosmic Patterns — Stars, Orbits, and the Geometry of Space

---

"The harmony of the world is made manifest in Form and Number, and the heart and soul and all the poetry of Natural Philosophy are embodied in the concept of mathematical beauty."
— Sir D'Arcy Wentworth Thompson

The patterns that govern the universe are not random. From the swirl of galaxies to the paths of planets, the cosmos follows precise, elegant, and often **geometric laws**. Ancient astronomers intuited this, while modern astrophysics now confirms it: **space is not empty chaos, but structured harmony**.

In this chapter, we explore how sacred geometry manifests on a **cosmic scale**, revealing that the same patterns found in flowers, shells, and temples also guide the stars, planets, and galaxies. Geometry, it turns out, is not just a tool for art or architecture — it is **the blueprint of the universe itself**.

I. The Celestial Code: A History of Cosmic Geometry

Human beings have long looked to the skies for meaning, rhythm, and pattern.

A. Ancient Cosmology

- **Babylonian, Egyptian, and Greek** astronomers saw celestial movement as divine mathematics.
- **Pythagoras** taught that the planets emitted sound based on their orbits — the "Music of the Spheres."
- Sacred texts such as the **Vedanga Jyotisha** in India described astronomical timekeeping in terms of nested cycles and geometric harmonies.

B. Astrology and Geometry

- Zodiacal systems divide the heavens into **12 equal parts**, rooted in **circular geometry**.
- Many ancient calendars were based on **geometric relationships** between solar and lunar cycles — e.g., the 19-year Metonic cycle.

II. The Geometry of Orbits: Ellipses and Harmonies

A. Kepler's Laws and Planetary Motion

Johannes Kepler discovered that:

1. Planets move in **elliptical orbits** (not perfect circles), with the sun at one focus.
2. The speed of a planet varies so that it sweeps out **equal areas in equal times**.
3. The square of a planet's orbital period is proportional to the cube of its average distance from the sun — a precise **mathematical ratio**.

These laws revealed that **geometry governs motion**, and that **orbits are sacred curves**.

B. Ellipses and Hidden Perfection

- An ellipse is a stretched circle and contains within it **perfect balance**.
- It reflects **duality and unity**: two focal points but one continuous path — a metaphor for many spiritual truths.

III. The Venus Pentagram: Celestial Harmony in Motion

One of the most stunning natural examples of cosmic geometry is the **pentagram formed by Venus** in its orbit relative to Earth.

A. What Is It?

- Over an 8-year cycle, Venus traces a **five-pointed star** (pentagram) in the sky as it aligns with Earth and the Sun.
- Each point corresponds to a **synodic conjunction**, where Venus passes between the Earth and Sun.

B. Geometric Significance

- The pentagram is associated with **Phi (Φ), the Golden Ratio**, found in each internal segment.
- Ancient cultures — especially the **Maya, Greeks, and Hermeticists** — viewed this pattern as symbolic of **cosmic balance and feminine divinity**.

IV. The Platonic Solids and the Cosmos

A. Kepler's Platonic Solar System

- Kepler tried to model the solar system using **nested Platonic solids** (tetrahedron, cube, octahedron, dodecahedron, icosahedron), believing they represented the orbits of the known planets.
- Though later disproven in detail, the underlying **geometric intuition was profound** — these shapes relate deeply to natural symmetry.

B. Cosmic Resonance

- These solids appear again in **quantum physics**, **molecular chemistry**, and **crystal lattices**.
- The **dodecahedron**, for example, was believed by Plato to represent the **shape of the universe** — and is now seen in cosmic background radiation patterns.

V. Galactic Spirals and the Fibonacci Sequence

A. Spiral Galaxies

- Roughly 70% of known galaxies are **spiral-shaped**, including the **Milky Way**.
- Their spiral arms follow **logarithmic spirals**, which often approximate the **Fibonacci sequence** or **Golden Ratio**.

B. Black Holes and Torus Geometry

- Black holes, though not fully understood, are believed to involve **toroidal dynamics** — a **donut-shaped geometry** found throughout energy systems, from atoms to galaxies.
- The **torus** is a symbol of **eternal return**, energy flow, and **dimensional gateways** — a central concept in both metaphysics and unified physics theories.

VI. Sacred Numbers in the Heavens

A. The Harmony of Constants

- **Pi (π)**, **Phi (Φ)**, and the **speed of light** are mathematical constants that appear repeatedly in cosmic measurements.
- The **distance between Earth and Sun**, the **size of the Moon**, and **planetary ratios** often reflect **harmonic patterns**.

B. The Sun, Earth, and Moon

- The Moon is **400 times smaller than the Sun** and **400 times closer to Earth** — allowing perfect total solar eclipses.
- These proportional "coincidences" form **mathematical synchronicities** that defy random explanation.

VII. Cosmic Geometry in Myth and Symbol

A. The Zodiac and the Circle of Life

- The Zodiac is a **geometric wheel**, divided into **12 signs** and **360 degrees** — mirroring the **circle, year,** and **human life cycle**.

B. The Tree of Life and Celestial Mapping

- In Kabbalistic mysticism, the **Tree of Life** is a **cosmic map** — often aligned with planetary energies and star constellations.
- Ancient star maps and megalithic structures (like **Stonehenge, Nabta Playa,** or **Newgrange**) aligned sacred spaces to **celestial events** through **geometric calculations**.

VIII. Fractals and the Expanding Universe

A. Fractal Cosmology

- Galaxies are not randomly scattered — they form **filaments and voids** that mirror **fractal branching**, like trees or neurons.
- **Self-similarity across scales** supports the ancient Hermetic principle: "As above, so below."

B. The Universe as a Hologram

- Some theories suggest the universe may be **holographic**, meaning all of reality could be encoded in a **two-dimensional geometric surface**.
- This would make sacred geometry not just metaphor, but **foundational to physical existence**.

IX. Summary: The Living Geometry of the Cosmos

From the path of Venus to the arms of galaxies, geometry is everywhere. Sacred geometry is not confined to Earth or to art — it is written in the stars.

- **Stars spiral. Planets dance. Orbits harmonize.**
- The cosmos is not just material — it is musical and mathematical.
- When we study sacred geometry, we are studying the **divine architecture of space itself**.

To look at the night sky with this awareness is to see **God's compass** in action — and to recognize ourselves not as observers, but as participants in a vast, geometric symphony.

Chapter 23: Sacred Geometry and the Chakras

"Geometry will draw the soul toward truth and create the spirit of philosophy."
— Plato

The chakras — energy centers within the human subtle body — are more than metaphors for emotional or psychological states. They are **spatially organized, vibrationally structured, and geometrically encoded** systems. Each chakra resonates with **a specific frequency, color, shape, and sacred geometric pattern** that corresponds to both energetic and physical realities.

In this chapter, we explore how **sacred geometry offers a visual, vibrational, and meditative map** to understanding and aligning the chakras. Through this lens, the chakras become more than just symbols — they become **keys to awakening multidimensional consciousness**.

I. The Chakra System: A Brief Overview

The chakra system originates from **ancient Vedic and Tantric traditions** of India and describes **seven primary energy centers** that run along the central column of the body (Sushumna Nadi), from the base of the spine to the crown of the head.

Each chakra:

- Corresponds to a **color** in the light spectrum
- Resonates with a **specific sound (bija mantra)**
- Is associated with a **particular element** (earth, water, fire, etc.)
- Governs **psychological, emotional, and spiritual states**
- Aligns with a **geometric archetype**

II. Geometry of the Chakras: Symbolism and Structure

Each chakra is traditionally depicted with a **lotus flower** — but hidden within those lotus designs are deeply **geometric mandalas**.

Let's examine each chakra and its sacred geometry:

1. Muladhara (Root Chakra)

- **Location:** Base of spine
- **Color:** Red
- **Element:** Earth
- **Sound:** Lam
- **Symbol:** 4-petaled lotus
- **Geometry: Square** — the shape of **stability, foundation, grounding**

Meaning:
The square symbolizes solidity, balance, and structure. This geometric root reflects our primal needs: survival, stability, and security. It is the **first building block** of consciousness.

---

2. Svadhisthana (Sacral Chakra)

- **Location:** Below the navel
- **Color:** Orange
- **Element:** Water
- **Sound:** Vam
- **Symbol:** 6-petaled lotus
- **Geometry: Circle with crescent moon** — associated with **fluidity and flow**

Meaning:
The **circle** represents the eternal and cyclical nature of energy. The crescent moon within symbolizes motion, creation, and sensuality — reflecting the emotional, creative, and reproductive forces of this chakra.

---

3. Manipura (Solar Plexus Chakra)

- **Location:** Upper abdomen
- **Color:** Yellow
- **Element:** Fire
- **Sound:** Ram
- **Symbol:** 10-petaled lotus
- **Geometry: Inverted Triangle** within a circle — symbol of **fire and transformation**

Meaning:
The downward-pointing **triangle** is a classical symbol of the element fire. It also denotes power directed inward, digestion, and **personal willpower**. It fuels transformation and identity.

4. Anahata (Heart Chakra)

- **Location:** Center of chest
- **Color:** Green
- **Element:** Air
- **Sound:** Yam
- **Symbol:** 12-petaled lotus
- **Geometry: Hexagram (Star of David)** — two intersecting triangles

Meaning:
The **hexagram** is the symbol of **balance and union** — male and female, above and below, spirit and matter. It is the perfect metaphor for the heart as the meeting place of body and soul, giving and receiving, love and forgiveness.

5. Vishuddha (Throat Chakra)

- **Location:** Throat
- **Color:** Blue
- **Element:** Ether (Space)
- **Sound:** Ham
- **Symbol:** 16-petaled lotus
- **Geometry: Circle inside a downward triangle**
- **Meaning:**
  The **circle** stands for the infinite potential of sound and vibration. The downward **triangle** once again symbolizes purification and clarity. The throat chakra is where **form becomes frequency** — thought becomes speech, intention becomes vibration.

6. Ajna (Third Eye Chakra)

- **Location:** Between the eyebrows

- **Color:** Indigo
- **Element:** Light / Mind
- **Sound:** Om
- **Symbol:** 2-petaled lotus
- **Geometry: Circle with two petals (or vesica piscis)**

Meaning:
The **Vesica Piscis** — two interlocking circles — symbolizes **duality merging into unity,** like the two hemispheres of the brain or the two eyes producing a single vision. This geometry activates insight, inner knowing, and spiritual perception.

---

7. Sahasrara (Crown Chakra)

- **Location:** Top of head
- **Color:** Violet or White
- **Element:** Consciousness
- **Sound:** Silence / Aum
- **Symbol:** 1,000-petaled lotus
- **Geometry: Infinite Circle / Fractal Pattern**

Meaning:
The **thousand-petaled lotus** is not just a number — it represents an **infinite unfolding**. The geometry of this chakra becomes fractal — every petal reflecting the whole. It is the union with the divine, the unmanifest, the geometry **beyond geometry**.

III. Chakras and the Flower of Life

Each chakra can be placed within the **Flower of Life** pattern — a multidimensional grid made up of interlocking circles — which reflects:

- **The unfolding of consciousness**
- **The nested nature of creation**

- **The harmonic spacing between chakras**

The **Seed of Life**, a subset of the Flower, can be aligned with the seven chakras, symbolizing the growth of consciousness from **formless unity** into **structured awareness**.

IV. Chakras, Sound, and Vibration

Geometry and frequency are deeply interwoven. Each chakra resonates at a **specific frequency** and responds to **vocal tones, musical notes, and mantras**.

Chakra	Note	Frequency (Hz)	Mantra	Shape
Root	C	256	Lam	Square
Sacral	D	288	Vam	Circle
Solar Plexus	E	320	Ram	Triangle
Heart	F	341.3	Yam	Hexagram
Throat	G	384	Ham	Circle
Third Eye	A	426.7	Om	Vesica Piscis
Crown	B	480	Silence	Fractal Lotus

By visualizing geometric shapes while intoning the associated mantra, practitioners can **activate and balance** these centers more effectively. This is the principle behind **Yantra meditation** — combining **shape, sound, and consciousness**.

V. Chakras and the Tree of Life

The Kabbalistic **Tree of Life** and the chakra system can be mapped together — both present **sacred paths of ascent**, aligning inner development with geometric order.

- **Chakras**: Seven energy centers of the body
- **Sefirot**: Ten spheres of divine emanation

Each chakra roughly corresponds to a **path on the Tree of Life**, showing how **East and West mirror each other** in sacred frameworks.

VI. Practical Applications: Healing and Alignment

A. Geometric Meditation

- Meditating on the **geometric shape of a chakra** can increase resonance and alignment.
- For example, visualizing a glowing hexagram at the heart can open the flow of unconditional love.

B. Chakra Yantras

- Yantras are **geometric diagrams** representing specific chakras and their energies.
- Used in **Tantric rituals**, they serve as portals for consciousness to access different frequencies of being.

C. Crystal and Color Geometry

- Each chakra is linked to **specific crystals** with geometric lattice structures (e.g., garnet for Root, amethyst for Crown).
- Arranging these stones in **sacred geometric layouts** can amplify their healing properties.

VII. Summary: The Geometry of Inner Alignment

The chakras are not just spiritual symbols — they are **geometric fields** within the human body. By understanding and working with their shapes, sounds, and patterns, we bring **our physical, emotional, mental, and spiritual bodies into harmony**.

When aligned:

- The **square of survival** becomes the **fractal of enlightenment**.
- Energy flows like **music made visible**.
- The body becomes a **temple of sacred form**.

Sacred geometry teaches us that we are not random beings — we are **living mandalas**, built in divine proportion, vibrating in sacred rhythm.

YANTRA OVERLAYS FOR THE SEVEN CHAKRAS

Chapter 24: Geometry of Time: Calendars, Cycles, and Synchronicity

"Time is the moving image of eternity."
— Plato, *Timaeus*

Time is not a straight line. It spirals, cycles, pulses, and echoes through reality like a vast, multidimensional rhythm. To the ancients, time was not just chronological — it was *sacred*. Its geometry could be measured in **orbits, seasons, solstices, and synchronicities** — all of which mirrored **cosmic order** and **divine design**.

In this chapter, we explore how civilizations across the world encoded **time into geometric structures**, and how understanding these patterns can awaken us to **a deeper synchronization with the universe**.

I. Time as Geometry

Time is traditionally seen as linear in the modern world — an arrow moving from past to future. But sacred traditions describe time as:

- **Cyclic**: Repeating seasons, moon phases, birth and death
- **Spiraled**: Evolutionary cycles that repeat but never in the same way
- **Fractal**: Patterns within patterns — days within weeks, months within years
- **Nested**: Micro and macro timelines (e.g., circadian rhythm vs. cosmic precession)

The **geometry of time** involves:

- **Circles** (cycles)
- **Spirals** (growth and evolution)
- **Vesica Piscis** (intersections of timelines)
- **Torus** (time-space as energy flow)

II. Ancient Calendars and Cosmic Design

Sacred calendars were built not just to track harvests, but to **align human life with celestial cycles**. Many were geometrically precise, encoded with knowledge of astronomy, rhythm, and divine proportion.

1. The Mayan Tzolk'in and Haab'

- The **Tzolk'in**: 260-day calendar, reflecting **gestation cycles**, Venus phases, and solar harmonics.
- The **Haab'**: 365-day solar calendar.
- Combined, they form the **Calendar Round**, a wheel of sacred time.

Geometric foundation: **Circular wheels within wheels**, and **vigesimal (base-20)** math patterns.

2. The Egyptian Solar Calendar

- Based on **heliacal rising of Sirius (Sopdet)**.
- Geometry used in **temple alignments** (e.g., Abu Simbel).
- Reflected in **sundials**, obelisks, and even pyramid shadow play.

3. The Vedic Yugas

- Four ages: Satya, Treta, Dvapara, Kali.
- Represented in geometric ratios (4:3:2:1).
- Time is cyclic and **measured in Mahayugas** (Great Ages) — billions of years.

4. The Hebrew Calendar and Tree of Life

- Lunar-solar hybrid calendar.
- Kabbalistic **Sefirot** represent both divine emanations and **sacred time cycles**.

III. Geometry in Seasonal and Astronomical Cycles

1. The Year as a Circle

- The solar year is a **360° cycle** (as visualized in the zodiac).

- Divided into **12 months, 4 seasons**, and **8 solar festivals** in pagan and Wiccan traditions (e.g., solstices, equinoxes, cross-quarter days).

2. The Moon and the Vesica Piscis

- Lunar cycles: new moon to full moon and back.
- **Synodic month:** 29.5 days.
- **Geometry:** Two intersecting circles — the vesica piscis — symbolize the overlap of **sun and moon** during eclipses.

3. Planetary Retrogrades and Sacred Loops

- Venus and Mercury trace **five-petaled flowers** across the sky (pentagonal geometry).
- These movements were tracked for millennia and considered **divine signatures** in the sky.

IV. The Spiral of Time and Conscious Evolution

The spiral is perhaps the most powerful geometry of time:

- **DNA coils**
- **Galactic arms**
- **Fibonacci spirals in nature**

Rather than repeating flatly, time **spirals upward** — each cycle bringing the opportunity for higher awareness.

Think of your life as a **spiral staircase** — each year brings you back to familiar themes but from a higher perspective.

V. Sacred Sites Aligned with Time

Sacred geometry was used in architecture to **track and celebrate time**:

- **Stonehenge (UK):** Aligned with solstices, built in concentric circles.
- **Newgrange (Ireland):** Winter solstice sunlight penetrates the inner chamber once a year.

- **Machu Picchu (Peru)**: Solstice alignment with Intihuatana Stone.
- **The Great Pyramid (Egypt)**: Encodes precessional data and stellar alignments.

These were not just monuments — they were **celestial clocks**, designed to resonate with **the breath of the cosmos**.

VI. Time, Synchronicity, and Consciousness

Carl Jung coined the term **synchronicity** to describe meaningful coincidences that defy linear causality. Sacred geometry teaches that:

- **All moments are connected** in an invisible web
- Geometries like the **Merkaba** (3D star tetrahedron) represent the **interdimensional matrix** in which time and space intersect
- Moments of synchronicity are **intersections of timelines**, symbolized by shapes like:
    - **Vesica Piscis** (intersecting lives or choices)
    - **Mandorla** (sacred intersection of heaven and earth)

VII. Personal Time Geometry

Understanding your **personal time cycles** can bring deeper harmony:

- **Birth charts** (astrology): geometric maps of planetary positions
- **Numerology**: your life path number reflects sacred arithmetic
- **Biorhythms**: physical, emotional, and intellectual cycles repeating every 23, 28, and 33 days respectively

You are not a passive observer of time — you are **a co-creator of its unfolding**.

VIII. Practices for Living in Sacred Time

1. **Observe Lunar Cycles**

- Set intentions on new moons, release on full moons.
- Use a **moon mandala** to track your emotions and creativity.

2. **Align with Solar Festivals**
    - Celebrate **solstices** and **equinoxes** with rituals, fasts, or feasts.
    - Recognize these days as energetic thresholds.

3. **Create a Personal Mandala Calendar**
    - Use a **circular template** to map your year, month, or life goals.
    - Visualize time as a wheel, not a list.

4. **Notice Synchronicities**
    - Keep a journal of "coincidences."
    - Meditate on **what geometry or cycle may be in play**.

The geometry of time is not only astronomical, but mystical. To step into **sacred time** is to live in harmony with the rhythms of the universe — to **awaken to patterns that echo through days, lives, and civilizations**.

Calendars are not just tools for scheduling — they are **maps of soul evolution**. By decoding the sacred geometry of time, we begin to **see eternity in the moment** and the **divine in the turning of every season**.

Part IV: Unlocking the Secrets — Applications and Inner Work

Chapter 25: Meditation with Sacred Geometry

"When the mind becomes still, the pattern of the cosmos reveals itself."
— Ancient Hermetic Teaching

Introduction: Geometry as a Gateway to Inner Stillness

Meditation is a practice of centering, focusing, and remembering the deeper order within and around us. Sacred geometry, with its perfect balance, symmetry, and mathematical grace, provides a **visual and energetic map** for this journey inward. It is more than a science or an art—it is a contemplative language that speaks directly to the soul.

In this chapter, we explore how sacred geometric forms—such as the Flower of Life, Metatron's Cube, mandalas, yantras, and Platonic solids—can be used as **tools for meditation**, leading to clarity, insight, and deep connection with the divine.

I. Why Meditate with Sacred Geometry?

A. Resonance with Universal Order

Geometric forms mirror the **harmonic structure of the cosmos**. When we meditate on them, our consciousness begins to resonate with:

- Balance
- Symmetry
- Proportion
- Unity

These qualities help align body, mind, and spirit.

B. Activating Archetypal Awareness

Geometric forms are **archetypes**—universal symbols that bypass the logical mind and speak directly to deeper levels of consciousness. Meditation with these symbols can:

- Awaken intuition
- Access higher dimensions of thought
- Heal fragmented perception

C. Anchoring Presence

Because geometry is **concrete and visible**, it serves as a powerful focus point in meditation—especially for visual learners or those who struggle with abstract stillness.

II. Preparatory Steps for Geometric Meditation

Before entering sacred geometric meditation, establish a supportive environment:

1. **Create Sacred Space**
    - Light a candle or incense.
    - Sit on a grounded surface or meditation cushion.
    - Place the chosen geometric image before you.
2. **Center the Breath**
    - Begin with deep diaphragmatic breathing.
    - Inhale for 4 counts, hold for 4, exhale for 4 (Box Breathing).
    - Let the mind settle and anchor in the body.
3. **Intention Setting**
    - Ask inwardly: "What am I seeking from this meditation?"
    - Clarity, healing, connection, peace?

III. Geometric Symbols and Their Meditative Qualities

1. The Flower of Life

Symbol of: Unity, interconnectedness, infinite creation
How to use:

- Gaze at the full pattern or trace it mentally with your eyes.
- Observe how all forms emerge from overlapping circles.
- Feel your own cells, breath, and thoughts syncing with the mandala of life.

Mantra: *"I am one with all that is."*

---

2. Metatron's Cube

Symbol of: Structure of the universe, divine intelligence, protection
How to use:

- Focus on the central hexagon or star tetrahedron.
- Visualize each Platonic solid unfolding from the central point.
- Use as a "visual prayer" for alignment with divine will.

Visualization: Imagine the cube rotating and activating each energy center (chakra).

---

3. The Sri Yantra

Symbol of: Union of the masculine and feminine; creation and dissolution
How to use:

- Begin from the outer square "gates," slowly drawing attention inward.
- Meditate on the nine interlocking triangles leading to the **bindu** (central dot).
- Breathe into the center, seeing it as the source of all manifestation.

Chant: "Aum" or "Shreem" (associated with abundance and the divine feminine).

---

4. Mandalas

Symbol of: Wholeness, self-reflection, cosmic blueprint
How to use:

- Color your own mandala as an active meditation.
- Let the symmetry guide your attention inward.
- Let the outer form mirror your inner landscape.

Practice: Focus on the outer ring, then progressively move toward the center.

---

5. Platonic Solids (3D Meditations)

Symbol of: Elements, balance, and multidimensional consciousness
How to use:

- Visualize each solid in your energy field.
    - Cube (Earth): Stability
    - Tetrahedron (Fire): Passion and clarity
    - Octahedron (Air): Balance and heart opening
    - Icosahedron (Water): Flow and emotion
    - Dodecahedron (Ether): Spirit and higher realms
- Rotate the shape mentally or "place" it around your aura.

Advanced Practice: Combine breathwork with the geometry—inhale the shape, exhale its light.

IV. Types of Geometric Meditation Practices

A. Gazing (Trataka)

- Sit in front of a geometric image (at eye level).
- Gaze steadily without blinking for several minutes.
- Close eyes and visualize the imprint behind the eyelids.
- Allow insight to rise from within.

Benefit: Improves concentration, opens third eye, sharpens perception.

B. Visualization

- Close eyes and build the geometric form in your inner vision.
- Start with a simple shape (like a triangle or spiral).
- Gradually progress to complex forms like Metatron's Cube or a torus.

Tip: Don't worry about "perfect" visuals. Focus on **sensation and energy flow**.

C. Guided Journey with Geometry

Use sacred geometry as a **portal** into an inner temple:

- Imagine entering a crystalline temple with geometric light structures.
- Move through sacred chambers shaped as Platonic solids.
- Meet spiritual guides or archetypal energies within.

Use prompts like:

- "What is the message of this shape for me today?"
- "What aspect of my life needs this symmetry?"

D. Breathing with Geometry

- Inhale while mentally tracing the edges of a shape (e.g., triangle = 3 beats).
- Exhale while tracing another layer.
- Align breath with spiral or toroidal flow.

Example: Visualize a torus and let the breath move in/out through the heart center.

V. Healing and Activation Through Geometric Meditation

Healing Applications

- Reduces anxiety and restores coherence
- Balances left-right hemispheres of the brain
- Strengthens the energy field (aura)
- Harmonizes chakras through geometric visualization

Activation Experiences

- Opening of higher consciousness or third eye
- Deep feelings of interconnection with all life
- Sudden insights or downloads of intuitive knowledge

VI. Integration: Living the Geometry

Meditation with sacred geometry is not only a practice of stillness, but a **recalibration of your way of seeing**. As you return to the external world:

- Observe shapes and patterns in nature with new eyes
- Decorate your space with geometric art or altars
- Infuse your creative work with symmetry and symbolism

Let the order you've internalized express itself in daily life. In doing so, you become a **living mandala**—a vessel of balance, beauty, and truth.

The geometric forms that guide the structure of galaxies also reside within you. Each time you meditate with sacred geometry, you realign with this divine design. Over time, the lines, spirals, and shapes reveal themselves not only as symbols, but as **you**—the conscious embodiment of the sacred pattern unfolding.

Chapter 26: Creating and Using Sacred Symbols

"Symbols are the language of the soul—bridges between the seen and the unseen."
— Manly P. Hall

Introduction: The Power of the Sacred Symbol

From the spiraling galaxies overhead to the spiraling DNA within us, the universe communicates in **patterns, proportions, and symbols**. Sacred symbols are not just decorative motifs—they are carriers of meaning, energy, and intention. When consciously created and activated, they become **living tools** for healing, meditation, manifestation, and alignment with divine order.

In this chapter, we will explore:

- What makes a symbol "sacred"
- How to design your own sacred symbols
- Traditional and modern uses
- Methods to charge, activate, and integrate symbols into daily life

---

I. What Are Sacred Symbols?

A **sacred symbol** is a geometric or abstract design imbued with spiritual, mystical, or metaphysical significance. Unlike arbitrary signs, sacred symbols are:

- **Archetypal**: they tap into universal patterns.
- **Energetic**: they carry and transmit frequencies.
- **Intentional**: created or used with conscious purpose.
- **Reflective**: mirrors of both the cosmos and the soul.

They can be simple (e.g., a circle, triangle, spiral) or complex (e.g., the Sri Yantra, Metatron's Cube, mandalas, or yantras).

II. The Geometry of Meaning: Understanding Symbolic Foundations

Before creating your own symbols, it helps to understand **core geometric forms** and what they signify:

Shape	Symbolic Meaning
Point	Origin, unity, divine spark
Line	Direction, connection, intention
Circle	Wholeness, eternity, inclusivity
Triangle	Trinity, transformation, stability
Square	Foundation, manifestation, earthly balance
Pentagon	Life, health, harmony (linked to Golden Ratio)
Hexagon	Structure, unity in diversity (e.g., beehive pattern)
Spiral	Growth, evolution, expansion
Vesica Piscis	Creation, duality, portal, sacred union

These are the **building blocks** of all sacred symbols.

III. The Act of Creation: Designing Your Own Sacred Symbols

Creating sacred symbols is a **spiritual art form**. The process itself becomes a meditation and an invocation.

Step 1: Clarify Intention

Ask yourself:

- What is this symbol for?
    - Protection? Healing? Focus? Transformation? Connection?
- Is it personal or collective?

Your **intention** will shape every design decision.

Step 2: Choose Your Geometry

Select foundational shapes based on your purpose:

- **Circle + triangle**: spiritual awakening
- **Square + spiral**: grounding with evolution

- **Vesica piscis + hexagon**: creative birth and harmony

You may also draw from existing sacred systems:

- **Yantras** (Indian)
- **Sigils** (Western magic)
- **Runes** (Nordic)
- **Ogham** (Celtic)

Step 3: Draw the Symbol

Use compass, straightedge, or digital design software. Steps:

1. Begin with a central point (the source).
2. Build symmetrical structures around it.
3. Use repetition, mirroring, or radial expansion.
4. Ensure **balance** and **proportion**—the energy flows best through order.

You may also trace or stylize existing forms (e.g., Seed of Life, platonic solids) and customize them.

Step 4: Add Layers of Meaning

- **Color**: Each hue carries vibration (e.g., blue = peace, red = passion).
- **Number**: Use sacred numbers like 3, 4, 7, 12, or 108.
- **Directionality**: Consider North–South–East–West orientation.
- **Words/Mantras**: Optionally embed key words, affirmations, or syllables.

Step 5: Activate the Symbol

- Place hands over it and **breathe intention** into the symbol.
- Use spoken word (e.g., "This symbol is now a conduit for peace").
- Expose it to **sunlight, crystals,** or **meditation energy**.
- Place it in a sacred space to build resonance.

IV. Traditional Uses of Sacred Symbols

1. In Meditation

- Gaze (Trataka) upon the symbol.
- Visualize it in the third eye.
- Place it under your seat or in your hands while sitting.

2. For Protection

- Wear as a talisman or pendant.
- Draw over thresholds, doors, or sacred containers.
- Use in ritual circles or around altars.

3. For Manifestation

- Design a symbol charged with your specific goal (e.g., abundance, healing).
- Place it under your pillow, journal, or workspace.
- Revisit it during your affirmations or intention-setting rituals.

4. In Ritual and Ceremony

- Paint or trace symbols on candles, water vessels, or cloth.
- Use symbols as sigils in spellwork or prayer rituals.
- Chant or tone while visualizing the symbol activating.

V. Advanced Symbol Creation Practices

A. Sigil Crafting (Western Occult Tradition)

1. Write your intention as a statement ("I am calm and centered").
2. Remove repeating letters.
3. Rearrange the remaining letters into a symbolic design.
4. Focus intensely on the sigil while meditating.
5. Release it from conscious thought—let it work through the subconscious.

B. Mandala Creation

- Begin from the center and build outward with repeating geometric motifs.
- Include colors, personal symbols, and numerology.
- Ideal for reflecting inner states or spiritual journeys.

C. Light Codes and Downloads

Some meditators intuitively "receive" symbols through dreams, altered states, or intuitive drawing.

- Trust the process.
- Journal what arises.
- Use these as **personal soul symbols**—they may not follow traditional rules but carry deep resonance.

VI. Working with Your Symbol Over Time

Symbols gain potency with **repetition, devotion, and integration**.

- **Meditate** with the symbol daily.
- **Dream** with it under your pillow.
- **Include** it in your artwork or creative expressions.
- **Share** it if you feel called—symbols can heal collectively.

Over time, the symbol becomes a **living entity**, a reflection of your spiritual path and energetic essence.

VII. Symbol Portals and Conscious Connection

Sacred symbols are **not static**—they are **interactive gateways**. When you connect deeply with one:

- It can **alter your consciousness**.
- It can offer **insight, clarity, or intuitive messages**.

- It can serve as a **bridge between worlds**—the known and the numinous.

Every symbol holds a **threshold**: a point where thought dissolves and the **language of the soul begins**.

To create a sacred symbol is to **externalize the divine spark within**. You become the artist, the mystic, and the mystic's mirror—bringing invisible truth into form. Your symbols carry your frequency, your prayer, your offering.

In a world hungry for depth and harmony, sacred symbols remind us that **meaning is not lost—it is encoded**, waiting to be revealed through line, color, shape, and intention.

When you draw or use a sacred symbol, you're not just making art—you're making **contact** with the eternal.

Chapter 27: Healing with Geometric Energy

"Geometry will draw the soul toward truth and create the spirit of philosophy."
— Plato

Introduction: The Geometry of Healing

In the dance between form and energy, geometry emerges as a bridge—one that connects the tangible and intangible, the physical body and the subtle energy fields. Just as crystals, sound frequencies, and color can affect well-being, so too can geometric forms. Sacred geometry, with its precise mathematical harmony, doesn't just represent healing—it **induces** it.

Healing with geometric energy is the application of intentional shapes, patterns, and energetic structures to **balance, realign,** and **awaken** the natural healing intelligence of the body and spirit. In this chapter, we explore how geometry can be used for emotional, energetic, and physical restoration.

I. Why Geometry Heals

A. Resonance and Coherence

- **Healthy systems** exhibit coherent, harmonious patterns.
- Illness often arises when those patterns become chaotic or distorted.
- Geometric forms restore **resonance** by projecting order into the field.

Just as a tuning fork can harmonize a discordant instrument, sacred geometry can **entrain** the energy body back into balance.

B. The Universal Language of Form

The body responds to symbols and shapes at a **subconscious level**. Cells and tissues naturally organize themselves according to geometric principles:

- **DNA coils** in spirals.
- **Cells divide** in hexagonal symmetry.
- **Organs** exhibit the Fibonacci sequence and golden ratios.

Healing with geometry works because it **speaks the same language** as the body's innate intelligence.

II. The Energetic Blueprint: Aura, Chakras, and Subtle Bodies

Healing geometry targets the **energy anatomy** of the human system:

1. The Aura

- Surrounds the body in layers, each corresponding to mental, emotional, and spiritual health.
- Geometric patterns (e.g. the Merkaba, Metatron's Cube) can be visualized or placed in the aura to stabilize it.

2. Chakras

- Each chakra has geometric associations (e.g., the root chakra with a square, the heart with a hexagram).

- Overlaying corresponding geometry on each energy center can stimulate or calm it.

3. Meridians and Nadis

- Subtle energy pathways that can be mapped using geometry.
- Sacred symbols help clear energetic blockages, much like acupuncture but vibrationally.

III. Geometric Tools for Healing

1. Platonic Solids

These five shapes correspond to the classical elements and function as energetic tuning forks:

Shape	Element	Use for Healing
Tetrahedron	Fire	Transformation, vitality
Cube	Earth	Grounding, stability, pain relief
Octahedron	Air	Breath, balance, emotional clarity
Icosahedron	Water	Flow, creativity, trauma release
Dodecahedron	Ether	Spiritual healing, higher connection

How to use:

- Hold or place around the body
- Visualize spinning or glowing within a chakra
- Use crystal forms shaped in these geometries

---

2. The Flower of Life

A master healing grid composed of overlapping circles symbolizing the interconnectedness of all life.

Applications:

- Place water, crystals, or food on the pattern to charge it with coherent energy.
- Meditate with the image to balance all energy centers.
- Trace the design over the body or aura with your hands or visualization.

---

3. Metatron's Cube

Contains all Platonic solids and represents divine structure and protection.

Healing Functions:

- Clear dense or dark energy from the field.
- Realign the nervous system and subtle body.
- Use in energy healing sessions as a scanning or balancing tool.

---

4. Mandalas and Yantras

Intricate symmetrical designs used for focusing the mind and aligning subtle energy fields.

Use in Healing:

- Color or create mandalas to express and transform emotion.
- Gaze (trataka) at a yantra to calm the nervous system and open higher chakras.
- Include mantras or healing affirmations within your mandala art.

---

5. Light and Crystal Grids

Crystals placed in sacred geometric patterns (e.g., star tetrahedrons, spirals, vesica piscis) can amplify healing intentions.

Techniques:

- Create a grid under a healing table or around a meditation space.
- Program each stone with a specific intention.

- Combine with Reiki, breathwork, or sound healing for multidimensional alignment.

IV. Healing Practices and Techniques

A. Visualization with Sacred Geometry

- Imagine spinning shapes (e.g., octahedron) at the location of discomfort.
- Visualize breathing in a specific pattern (e.g., a golden spiral into the heart).
- Let the form "absorb" or "realign" dissonant energy.

B. Water Charging with Geometry

- Water holds memory and responds to shape.
- Place a water bottle over a printed sacred pattern (like the Flower of Life).
- Leave it in sunlight or moonlight for several hours.
- Drink mindfully to integrate geometric frequency into your cells.

C. Hands-On Healing with Geometry

- Draw a triangle, cube, or spiral over the body with your hands.
- Use your palm chakras to trace light patterns.
- Visualize light filling the shape as you direct it to a targeted area.

D. Breathing the Pattern

- Inhale tracing one side of a triangle or point of a star.
- Exhale through another.
- Continue in cycles, using the breath to "build" the form inside you.

V. Emotional and Mental Healing with Symbols

Certain shapes can gently release or reframe emotional patterns:

Shape/Pattern	Emotional Effect
Spiral (inward)	Self-reflection, clarity
Spiral (outward)	Expression, letting go
Hexagon	Harmony, community, trust
Triangle (upward)	Empowerment, confidence
Circle	Wholeness, safety

Use these as journaling prompts, therapeutic art, or energetic focal points in healing sessions.

VI. Sound and Geometry: Healing Through Frequency and Form

- Sound vibrations naturally form geometric patterns (as seen in cymatics).
- Chanting mantras while visualizing geometry enhances both practices.
- Singing bowls or binaural beats can be paired with geometric visualization to deepen healing.

Example:

- Chant "OM" while gazing at a Sri Yantra.
- Visualize the sound rippling outward in golden spirals from your heart.

VII. Integrating Geometric Healing into Daily Life

- Decorate spaces with sacred patterns to subtly influence mood and energy.
- Wear or carry amulets with symbols like the Seed of Life or Metatron's Cube.
- Start each day with a 5-minute geometry meditation to align mind, body, and spirit.

Affirmation Practice:
"As I align with sacred geometry, I restore my inner harmony and remember the perfection of my being."

Healing with geometric energy is not just about symbols—it's about **remembering your place in the larger pattern**. As you attune to the language of shape, number, and frequency, you come into resonance with the great design of the cosmos—and your body responds.

Geometry heals not by force, but by **invitation**. It invites your body and spirit to recall what it already knows: that it was born from symmetry, balance, and sacred intention.

By working with these patterns, you become not just a recipient of healing—but a **conduit for harmony** in your own life and in the lives of others.

Chapter 28: Personal Transformation Through Pattern Awareness

"The pattern is the path."
— Anonymous Hermetic Teaching

Introduction: Awakening to the Pattern Within

From the spiral of a seashell to the double helix of DNA, sacred patterns permeate all levels of existence. As we begin to **see these patterns** not only in nature and geometry but also in our own thoughts, behaviors, and life experiences, something powerful happens: we awaken to the **deep coherence** that underlies our lives.

This chapter explores how becoming aware of patterns—visual, emotional, energetic, and behavioral—can catalyze profound **personal transformation**. Through sacred geometry, pattern recognition becomes a mirror, a tool, and ultimately a spiritual path.

I. The Nature of Patterns: Mirrors of the Self

A. Patterns as Reflections

Patterns are repetitive structures, both visible and invisible, that reveal consistency in form or behavior. In personal development:

- Habits are behavioral patterns.
- Emotional cycles are energetic patterns.
- Belief systems are mental constructs following archetypal patterns.

By identifying these, we gain **insight into our inner architecture**.

B. The Principle of As Above, So Below

Sacred geometry teaches that what is true in the macrocosm is true in the microcosm. Recognizing the **patterns in nature and cosmos** can help us understand and heal the **patterns in our psyche and life journey**.

II. Seeing Patterns in Daily Life

A. Behavioral and Emotional Loops

- Do you attract similar relationships?
- Do you face repeated challenges in work or health?
- Are there emotions or reactions that occur predictably?

These repetitions often point to a **core pattern** seeking your attention and transformation.

B. Synchronicities and Recurring Symbols

The universe communicates through **symbols and synchronicities**—number sequences, animals, dreams, or events that echo geometric harmony. Paying attention to these is part of cultivating **pattern awareness**.

III. Sacred Geometry as a Tool for Inner Mapping

Sacred geometry is not just about external forms—it also functions as an **inner diagnostic system**.

A. Shapes and the Psyche

- **The Circle** may symbolize completeness or entrapment, depending on your relationship with wholeness.
- **The Triangle** could represent your relationship with power, duality, and balance.
- **The Spiral** reveals how you grow: do you ascend consciously or spiral into old patterns?

These shapes can be used in journaling, meditation, or therapy to **identify personal patterns and shifts**.

B. The Mandala as a Mirror

Carl Jung viewed the mandala as a symbol of the self. Creating or reflecting on mandalas can reveal:

- Emotional states
- Inner conflicts
- Desires for integration or healing

IV. Transformation Through Conscious Pattern Work

Once patterns are seen, they can be reshaped.

A. The Alchemy of Awareness

The first step in transformation is awareness. The moment you name and witness a repeating pattern—without judgment—you create space for change.

Use reflective questions:

- What pattern am I repeating?
- Where does it originate?
- What lesson is it offering me?

B. Rewriting the Pattern

Sacred geometry offers templates for realignment:

- Replace chaos with **the Flower of Life** (wholeness).
- Replace fear with **the triangle** (stability).
- Replace indecision with **the spiral** (growth).

Visualization, breathwork, and symbolic drawing can help "install" new patterns in the subconscious.

C. Emotional Healing with Pattern Interruption

Interrupting unhealthy emotional loops is key to healing.

- Use geometric breath (square or triangle breathing) to calm the nervous system.
- Meditate on symmetrical forms to bring balance to chaotic thinking.
- Draw sacred shapes as a form of self-regulation and emotional release.

V. Living in Alignment: Becoming a Living Mandala

A. Daily Practices for Pattern Integration

- Start your day with a **geometric visualization** (e.g., breathing through a golden spiral).
- Use a **symbol of the week** (like the Vesica Piscis) to guide decisions and reflections.
- **Journal in mandala form**: write in circles or draw shapes to express experiences.

B. Creating a Personal Pattern Map

Craft a visual map of your life's patterns:

- What themes repeat in love, health, purpose?
- What sacred geometric forms represent those themes?
- What new patterns do you want to create?

Use this as a sacred altar or vision board.

VI. Case Studies in Transformation

1. Emma – Breaking the Circle of Self-Sabotage

Emma noticed her tendency to start creative projects and abandon them. She worked with the **circle** in meditation and dreamwork, realizing she feared completion due to childhood rejection. By replacing her inner circle with **a spiral**, she began to see her progress as non-linear and evolving, not failing.

2. Leo – Awakening to the Star Within

After three failed relationships with emotionally unavailable partners, Leo meditated on the **hexagram (Star of David)**, representing the union of opposites. He realized he was attracting what he hadn't integrated: his own vulnerability. His relationships changed after he did.

VII. The Fractal Path: Evolution in Cycles

Life is not linear—it's fractal. We revisit the same patterns at different levels of growth. This means:

- Old challenges re-emerge, but with new awareness.
- Each return offers refinement, not failure.

The spiral becomes our teacher. We evolve through **repetition with awareness**.

When you understand the patterns of your own mind, emotions, and actions, you begin to shape reality from the **inside out**. Sacred geometry offers not just symbols—but tools for mastery.

Pattern awareness is not about perfection. It's about becoming conscious of what governs your life and choosing, again and again, to realign with harmony, truth, and love.

When you see yourself as part of the grand design, you no longer feel broken—you feel **woven** into the sacred pattern of creation.

Chapter 29: Drawing the Divine — Practical Exercises and Visual Practices

"When you draw a sacred form, you draw the essence of the universe into yourself."
— Ancient Hermetic Maxim

Introduction: Creation as Meditation

Drawing sacred geometry is more than art—it's a **form of devotion**, a way of aligning your consciousness with the order of the cosmos. As your compass traces a circle or your ruler connects symmetrical lines, your mind begins to quiet, your breath slows, and you enter a meditative state. This chapter is about reclaiming this ancient practice—not as a technical task, but as a **spiritual discipline**.

In this space of line and form, you are both **artist and alchemist**—transforming chaos into order, emotion into clarity, and vision into manifestation.

I. Why Draw Sacred Geometry?

A. Embodying Divine Intelligence

- The act of drawing geometric forms is a kinesthetic prayer.
- It brings intellectual understanding into physical embodiment.
- Each mark is a **gesture of alignment** with higher order.

B. Visual Harmony as Healing

- Creating symmetry on the page generates internal harmony.
- The focus required develops **concentration and stillness**.
- Drawing trains the brain toward **pattern recognition and intuitive clarity**.

II. Tools and Materials

You don't need to be an artist—just committed and curious. Here's what to gather:

Tool	Use
Compass	Drawing circles and arcs
Ruler/Straightedge	Drawing precise lines and connections
Protractor	Measuring angles (especially for yantras)
Pencil and Eraser	Initial sketches and corrections
Fine Pen/Marker	For inking final drawings
Colored Pencils	Enhancing emotional and symbolic meaning
Drawing Pad	Smooth, heavy paper ideal for geometry

Optional:

- Graph paper for beginners
- Golden Ratio calipers
- Compass extension arm for large-scale drawings

III. Foundational Drawing Exercises

Exercise 1: The Circle (Unity & Infinity)

1. Place your compass point.
2. Draw a single, slow circle.
3. Contemplate its wholeness and your connection to all that is.
4. Breathe deeply as you complete each arc.

Meditation prompt: "Where in my life can I return to center?"

Exercise 2: The Vesica Piscis (Creation)

1. Draw a circle.

2. Keeping the same compass width, place the point on the edge of the circle.
3. Draw a second circle, overlapping the first.
4. The almond-shaped space between is the **Vesica Piscis**.

Reflection: This shape represents **birth, duality, and sacred union**.

Exercise 3: Seed of Life

1. Begin with a circle.
2. Continue adding six overlapping circles around the original, forming a flower-like structure.
3. Keep your compass width constant for all.

Meaning: The Seed of Life represents the **seven stages of creation**.

IV. Intermediate Patterns

Exercise 4: Flower of Life

1. Begin with the Seed of Life.
2. Add another ring of circles around the perimeter.
3. Keep extending in layers to create the full Flower of Life.

Tip: Use light pencil lines and trace over final segments with ink.
Contemplation: What is my relationship to the whole?

Exercise 5: Metatron's Cube

1. Begin with the Flower of Life.
2. Identify the **13 key points** of intersecting circles.
3. Use a ruler to connect all points to one another.
4. You'll reveal **all Platonic solids** nested within.

Symbolism: Metatron's Cube is the **blueprint of creation** and divine structure.

Exercise 6: Sri Yantra

1. Draw a central upward triangle.
2. Continue layering alternating upward and downward triangles, increasing in size and maintaining alignment to the central bindu (dot).
3. Add lotus petals, the square base (bhupura), and concentric circles.

Note: This is an advanced form. Use a protractor and fine tools.
Meditation: Gaze at your yantra and chant "Om" to activate the image.

V. Drawing for Meditation and Healing

A. Mandala Creation

- Start with a circle.
- Divide it into even segments (6, 8, or 12).
- Build symmetrical patterns from the center outward using shapes, curves, and layers.
- Color with intention (use color theory or chakra correspondence).

Practice: Each mandala is a mirror of your current state. Allow it to unfold organically.

B. Breath and Drawing Integration

1. As you draw each stroke, coordinate with your breath.
    - Inhale before each line
    - Exhale as you draw
2. Let each shape reflect a **breath cycle**, syncing inner and outer rhythm.

C. Drawing and Emotion

- Angry or tense? Draw triangles or spirals.
- Feeling scattered? Work with squares or hexagons.
- Need to forgive? Use circles and mandalas.
- Seeking creativity? Try the golden spiral.

VI. Color, Symbolism, and Intention

Color adds emotional and symbolic dimension:

Color	Quality	Use In Practice
Red	Grounding, strength	Root chakra, square grids
Blue	Calm, communication	Mandalas, Flower of Life
Gold	Divine light, higher wisdom	Sri Yantra, spirals, Metatron's Cube
Green	Heart, balance, healing	Hexagons, Seed of Life

Intention setting: Before drawing, write a word or phrase (e.g., "clarity," "peace") in the margin. Let it guide your pattern and colors.

VII. Final Practice: Personal Sacred Geometry Sigil

Create a symbolic geometric design that reflects your own energy signature:

1. Meditate on your core values or soul essence.
2. Choose 2–3 shapes that reflect this (e.g., triangle for transformation, circle for unity).
3. Layer them in a unique, harmonious way.
4. Add a central point (bindu) to represent your soul.
5. Optionally, inscribe a mantra or affirmation in the border.

Result: You now have your personal sacred geometry emblem—a **visual talisman** of your spiritual essence.

VIII. Using Your Drawings

- Place them on your altar or meditation space.
- Use them as **meditation focal points** (trataka).
- Gift them with blessings to loved ones.
- Hang them where their energy subtly affects your environment.
- Use them as **sigils** for manifestation or prayer.

To draw sacred geometry is to remember that you are both **creator and creation**. You are not merely reproducing forms—you are invoking archetypes, tracing divine memory, and aligning your body and spirit with the harmony that underpins all things.

When you draw the divine, you're not just putting pen to paper. You're participating in the cosmic act of creation. You're restoring beauty to your inner world. You're becoming the artist of your own sacred path.

Chapter 30: Living in Harmony with the Divine Pattern

"When we align our lives with the rhythm of the cosmos, we become living mandalas—wholeness made visible."
— Ancient Vedic Wisdom

Introduction: Geometry as a Way of Life

Sacred geometry is more than a set of mathematical constructs or beautiful diagrams. It is a **living intelligence**—a pattern that underlies all life, from galaxies to garden flowers, from DNA to human destiny. To understand sacred geometry is to remember that life itself is patterned, rhythmic, ordered, and **divinely intelligent**.

This chapter invites you to take sacred geometry off the page and into your body, mind, relationships, home, work, and spiritual path. This is where sacred geometry moves from art to **embodiment**—where knowledge becomes **wisdom**.

I. Understanding Harmony: The Essence of the Pattern

A. What Is Harmony?

Harmony is a dynamic balance between elements, much like the golden ratio in nature or the symmetrical precision of a mandala. In life, harmony means:

- Living in integrity with your values.
- Making space for both structure and flow.
- Honoring cycles of growth, rest, and renewal.

B. The Sacred Pattern as a Life Template

The divine pattern, as revealed through sacred geometry, teaches:

- **Balance** through symmetry (e.g., yin and yang).
- **Growth** through spirals and cycles.
- **Wholeness** through circles and mandalas.
- **Interconnectedness** through overlapping forms like the Flower of Life.

These aren't just symbolic—they are **instructional** for how to live well.

II. Attuning Your Inner Life

A. Emotional Resonance

Your emotions have frequency. Like harmonious geometry, balanced emotions flow smoothly and express coherence.

Practices to align emotion with sacred pattern:

- Meditate with geometric visuals (e.g., triangle for clarity, circle for calm).

- Use sound (chanting, tuning forks) with sacred intervals (e.g., the 432 Hz scale).
- Track emotional cycles like lunar phases or energetic spirals.

B. Mental Clarity Through Pattern Recognition

Disordered thinking leads to internal chaos. Sacred geometry teaches the mind to:

- Prioritize order without rigidity.
- Think in **systems and relationships** rather than isolated facts.
- Balance logic (masculine principle) with intuition (feminine principle).

Practice: Solve a geometric puzzle or mandala when you feel overwhelmed—it brings coherence to the brain.

III. Embodying the Pattern

A. The Body as a Sacred Form

Your body is a living example of sacred geometry:

- Proportions follow the Golden Ratio.
- Organs spiral and branch in fractal forms.
- The chakra system aligns along a central axis like a tree of life.

Embodiment Practices:

- **Yoga and Qigong** to activate sacred alignment.
- Walk in circular labyrinths to reflect your internal journey.
- Practice breathwork in geometric rhythms (e.g., box breathing: inhale-hold-exhale-hold in equal parts).

B. Movement in Sacred Space

- Arrange your home or altar using geometric principles (Feng Shui, Mandala orientation).

- Dance with intention: spiral, sway, and move in geometrically inspired choreography.
- Use **body tracing** of sacred forms like the pentagram (arms, legs, head) for energetic balancing.

IV. Harmonizing Relationships

A. Relationships as Geometric Fields

Each connection we form creates an **energetic field**—a geometric space of exchange:

- Triadic patterns in friendships, families, and teams reflect the stability or instability of a triangle.
- Vesica Piscis illustrates two overlapping souls birthing shared experience.

Reflection: Is your relationship pattern balanced? Are you repeating unconscious geometry—like entanglements instead of harmonies?

B. Sacred Communication

- Listen in spirals, not straight lines. Let the other's words lead you inward and back outward.
- Mirror the **geometry of respect**: equal spacing, eye contact, presence.
- Set boundaries with the clarity of a square and the warmth of a circle.

V. Living Cyclically and Naturally

A. Time as a Spiral, Not a Line

Modern culture treats time as linear. Sacred geometry reveals it as spiral or cyclical:

- Life moves in **seasons, rhythms, orbits**.
- Align with **moon phases, solstices, equinoxes**, and personal energy cycles.

Practice: Track your moods, dreams, or productivity with lunar or solar calendars to discover your natural rhythm.

B. Sacred Routine

Create a life rhythm that reflects geometric harmony:

- Morning: Focus inward (circle).
- Midday: Act with purpose (triangle).
- Evening: Reflect and release (spiral or wave).

Even your meals, sleep, and creative time can reflect **balance and proportion**.

VI. Designing Your Environment

A. Sacred Spaces

Design your home or workspace to reflect divine geometry:

- Use circular or octagonal shapes for meditation areas.
- Hang the **Flower of Life**, **Sri Yantra**, or **Metatron's Cube** in focal areas.
- Use light, symmetry, and natural proportions to promote flow and peace.

B. Nature as a Teacher

Spend time in forests, oceans, and gardens where **fractal geometry** abounds. Notice:

- Branching trees (dendritic patterns)
- Spiral shells and buds (Fibonacci sequence)
- Starry skies and crystal forms (Platonic solids)

Daily Practice: Observe one geometric pattern in nature and journal its metaphor for your life.

VII. Becoming the Pattern

When you consistently observe, meditate on, and live by the divine pattern, something beautiful happens: **you become it**.

You become the center of your own mandala, radiating wholeness. You respond rather than react. You move with purpose. You recognize life as art and spirit as architecture. Your intuition sharpens, your creativity expands, and your life becomes an expression of cosmic truth.

The divine pattern is not something to master—it is something to **remember**. It has always been with you, coded into your cells, your breath, your heartbeat, and your thoughts. Sacred geometry has been your silent companion since birth, whispering the language of wholeness.

To live in harmony with the divine pattern is to:

- Align your life with the flow of the universe.
- Live deliberately, cyclically, and beautifully.
- Reclaim your place in the great web of creation—not as an outsider, but as a conscious participant.

Let your thoughts be symmetrical, your actions be graceful, and your life be a mandala of meaning.

Printed in Dunstable, United Kingdom